Habits of the Balkan Heart

To Dianne,
With eternal
and deep-felt thanks
Hipe Meštrović
8-11-99

Habits of the Balkan Heart

SOCIAL CHARACTER
AND THE FALL OF COMMUNISM

By Stjepan G. Meštrović
with Slaven Letica and Miroslav Goreta

Texas A&M University Press
College Station

Frontispiece: "Mother Meditating," by Ivan Mestrovic, marble, 1930,
Zagreb, Croatia.

The paper used in this book meets the minimum requirements
of the American National Standard for Permanence
of Paper for Printed Library Materials, Z39.48–1984.
Binding materials have been chosen for durability.

Library of Congress Cataloging-in-Publication Data

Mestrovic, Stjepan Gabriel.
   Habits of the Balkan heart : social character and the fall of
Communism / Stjepan G. Meštrović with Slaven Letica and
Miroslav Goreta. — 1st ed.
      p.   cm.
   Includes bibliographical references (p.   ) and index.
   ISBN 0-89096-556-0. — ISBN 0-89096-593-5 (pbk.).
   1. Balkan Peninsula—Social conditions.   2. Political
culture—Balkan Peninsula.   3. Post-communism—Balkan
Peninsula.   I. Letica, Slaven.   II. Goreta, Miroslav.
III. Title.
HN613.5.M47   1993
306'.09496—dc20   93-11072
                                                           CIP

Contents

Preface

Our purpose in this book is to engage in a cultural interpretation of the collapse of Communism in the former Yugoslavia. We apply the notion "social character" as popularized by Alexis de Tocqueville (1845), Thorstein Veblen (1899), Erich Fromm (1955), David Riesman (1950), Robert N. Bellah (1985), and Seymour Martin Lipset (1989), among others, to a new setting. We do so through a reexamination of Dinko Tomašić's studies of Dinaric social character and through finding sociological affinities among these and other cultural analysts.

This new theoretical mix and new application of existing but frequently unconnected approaches to the study of culture lead to unexpected insights, interpretations, and tentative hypotheses that we hope will be useful to a wide audience that might include sociologists, historians, political scientists, as well as laypersons and students trying to make sense of the brutal current war in the former Yugoslavia. For example, we hold that Communism was never just the abstract antithesis to capitalism, and that Communism did not really expire, as claimed by Zbigniew Brzezinski (1989) and Francis Fukuyama (1992). On the contrary, we suggest that Communism in the former Yugoslavia was rooted in a fierce social character that preceded it, and that following the much-touted fall of Communism in the late 1980s, this type of social character may yet transform itself into another autocratic system that will be every bit as harsh and autocratic as Communism ever could be. Moreover, Communism in the former Yugoslavia was a disguised Serbian attempt to impose a Greater Serbia and was understood as such by the other republics in the former Yugoslavia. When the Communist ideology began to collapse in the late 1980s, all of the former Yugoslav republics except Montenegro seized the opportunity to free themselves from Serbian oppression. In response to these freedom movements, the Belgrade government reinforced its hard-line leanings and engaged in a pitiless war against its neighbors, in its openly proclaimed quest to establish a Greater Serbia.

Ours is not an empirical study, strictly speaking, although it is intended to illuminate and make sociological sense of empirical events in post-Communist Yugoslavia that many Western analysts as well as laypersons have found baffling. For example, we contend that Tomašić's studies of Yugoslav social character offer a sobering alternative to the West's unrealistic euphoria and naive optimism that capitalism and democracy would easily and quickly supplant Communism. Moreover, Tomašić predicted in 1948 the brutality, deceit, and white heat of hatred that did in fact emerge in the war that began in the former Yugoslavia in 1991. Had Western analysts known of or read Tomašić, perhaps they would have anticipated the long string of broken promises and cease-fires that have characterized the West's diplomatic dealings with the Belgrade regime in the early 1990s. The West was provincial to assume that all cultures in the world hold the same values that it holds dear, such as rational self-interest, keeping one's word, or honoring a contract. Finally, our study suggests that Western analysts are naive to regard Communism as somehow mysteriously self-begotten. It should be obvious that even Communism must have had cultural roots and that certain sorts of culture allowed Communism to become dominant. It is interesting that thousands of studies have followed Max Weber's ([1904] 1958) study of the cultural origins of capitalism, yet Tomašić's (1948b, 1953) studies of the cultural origins of Communism have been largely ignored. We contend that this is a blind spot in Western thinking that needs to be corrected.

Having summarized our argument, we shall not repeat any

portions of it in this preface. However, we would like to anticipate here some critical responses to our approach and to deflect some unwanted conclusions that some readers might wish to attribute to us. We anticipate this negative approach because a discussion such as ours necessarily raises issues of objectivity and because the notion of social character is held to be politically incorrect, or worse, in some sociological circles, even though Bellah, Riesman, Lipset, and other popular theorists use it.

With regard to objectivity, we note that as of late 1992, most of the world's nations and international organizations had singled out and condemned Serbia and Montenegro for their aggression and brutality against their neighbors. We feel that the history of the war in the former Yugoslavia since 1991 vindicates our criticisms of the Serbian government. The Belgrade regime headed by Slobodan Milošević clearly has demonstrated racism, expediency, a ruthless will to power, and a disregard for the West's ethical standards, as evidenced by all the cease-fire violations, the bombing of civilian targets, and other acts that have rightly been condemned by the West as crimes against humanity. To be sure, the Croats and Bosnians have also engaged in war crimes, yet the world's collective consciousness has concluded clearly that the overwhelming preponderance of the human rights abuses were perpetrated by the Belgrade regime.

Having noted our broad agreement with world opinion, however, we lament that the notion of collective responsibility is problematic and undeveloped in Western thought, which, because of its utilitarian tradition, tends to be oriented toward the individual. One of Durkheim's foremost disciples, Paul Fauconnet, wrote a sociological treatise on collective responsibility in 1920, but it has not been translated from French and has had practically no impact among sociologists, diplomats, or lawyers. Our point is that in criticizing the inhumane policies of the Milošević regime, we do not mean to extend that criticism to all Serbs. Moreover, we point to another blind spot in Western social theory. In an era that commonly punishes whole peoples for the acts of their leaders (such as the case of Iraq and Saddam Hussein), how does one affix collective responsibility with any degree of genuine justice? We pose this as a serious problem that Western intellectuals need to address.

As for the notion of social character, we would like to be read and understood strictly in relation to the distinguished theorists we cite as using this term, from Tocqueville to Lipset. It would be wrong for readers to impose their own agenda regarding this term onto our usage or to attribute sinister misunderstandings that stem from this term and its synonyms. Specifically, we do not wish to imply any sort of biological factors in social character; we do not mean that social character is evenly distributed throughout a society; and we do not mean to imply that social character is permanently fixed or that it cannot be changed. What we do maintain is that, as developed by Erich Fromm (1955), social character is a substitute for biological instinct among humans; that social character explains the diversity among the world's many cultures; that social character in each culture has its good as well as its bad aspects, and that these distinctions are themselves culturally relative; and that meaningful change can occur when one takes social character into account, not if one pretends that it does not exist.

The notion of social character and its derivatives hold an ambiguous place in the sociological profession. On the one hand, as already noted, some of sociology's most distinguished theorists have made use of this concept and its equivalents (collective consciousness, habits of the heart), from Tocqueville to Lipset. On the other hand, the notion of social character is deemed as nonsociological and politically incorrect by many contemporary sociologists. This is probably because this concept implies differences among groups of people in a postmodern era that stresses the end of difference (Baudrillard 1986). However, such a position cannot account for the many real differences that are found among the world's ethnic groups and that often erupt in violence. We cannot, and do not hope to, resolve this conflict in this book, realizing that we will never convince readers who are hostile to this concept to read us with an open mind. All we can do is note that we are aware of the controversy engendered by the use of the concept of social character, that we lament that it has divided sociologists, and that if a hidden agenda must be attributed to us in relying on this concept, it is an agenda geared toward democracy and liberalism. We do not believe that the cause of liberal democracy is promoted by pretending that the world is homogeneous, when it clearly is not.

Additionally, we would like to observe that whereas the notion of social character is problematic for contemporary sociologists, it is in fact implied by laypersons as well as politicians in common, everyday usage. If cultural differences did not exist, one could not explain how tourists attribute French culture to the French, differences between Croatians and Germans, or the host of other distinctions that must be made by world travelers if they are to survive their journeys. As for the world's politicians, they routinely refer to nations as if these political entities possessed qualities that are normally attributed to human actors. Thus, President Bush refers to characteristic American compassion for the underdog; former Prime Minister Margaret Thatcher used to refer to Germany as the Hun; Prime Minister Mulroney refers to the history of friendship between Canada and the United States—and so on. Again, these differences among the world's nations seem to count much more heavily than the ill-conceived illusions that tried to suppress ethnic or national differences, from Communism to the increasingly problematic quest for a United States of Europe.

Our use of the notion of social character is not meant to be analytic. For example, we do not and cannot account for the predatory aspects of the Dinaric types of Slavs. We do not explain why much of former Yugoslavia lacks a liberal tradition that is taken for granted by many Western nations. We offer no blueprint for how the negative aspects of the social character that we treat might be changed to a more democratic type. In fact, we would point out that these and related analytic issues betray a Western, Weberian provincialism that assumes the supreme importance of rational cause-and-effect relations in explaining phenomena that are not taken for granted by the entire world.

By contrast, our contribution is much more modest, straight-forward, and possibly more useful to policymakers than to acade-micians. We argue that regardless of its origins, the barbaric aspects of Dinaric social character must be taken seriously because they portend the possible transformation of Communism into a new strain of totalitarianism. We imply that because much of Yugoslavia lacks a credible liberal tradition, the United States, France, Great Britain, and other nations with such a tradition should realize that newly freed nations live the democratic dream through them, vi-cariously. In this regard, we criticize Western nations for their slow response to help post-Communist nations who wanted to join the Western orbit of cultural values. Finally, we contend that democ-racy will take hold in some post-Communist nations and portions of the former Yugoslavia through strenuous effort and self-conscious, collective examination of their social characters. One should not expect otherwise. After all, individuals who seek to change neurotic or otherwise destructive character traits often have to endure years of psychotherapy and must work hard to change their habits. Why should it be any easier for entire peoples who have suffered under the collective neurosis of Communism?

Finally, some sociologists will probably object to our delib-erately combining the insights of seemingly bona fide sociologists such as Thorstein Veblen with the historian Oswald Spengler, the literary critic and historian Henry Adams, and other apparent non-sociologists. Our reply is that sociology was established about a century ago by intellectuals who were trained in philosophy, his-tory, economics, and the other disciplines that preceded sociology. In fact, there did not exist any truly bona fide classical founders of sociology because sociology is a renegade discipline. In going back to the roots of sociology, we were forced to deal with these other approaches to human culture. We would like to believe that our approach will enrich sociological theory, not simply make our colleagues defensive.

Having clarified our intentions in writing this book, we would like to emphasize the distinctive aspects of the present study. In chapter 1, we trace the notion of social character and its synonyms. In chapter 2, we point out that Yugoslavia was an artificial construction of several cultures and that there have been at least five separate Yugoslavias in the twentieth century. The notion of social character that we introduce leads naturally to a comparison and contrast between Tocqueville's and Tomašić's depictions of American and South Slavic social characters, respectively. Thus, chapter 3 leads to the insight that much like the victory of the North over the South in the American Civil War was a decisive cultural event, the possible victory of Serbia in the current Balkan war would also constitute much more than a military victory. An entire cultural worldview is at stake.

Chapter 4 takes up another dimension that flows logically from our analysis, namely, the similarities and differences between Serbian imperialism and German imperialism in this century. Thorstein Veblen and Oswald Spengler are key analysts in such a discussion, and the German connection is important again because of Germany's support for Croatia and Slovenia against Serbia. Finally, in chapter 5 we take up an issue that concerns many laypersons: How could a war as brutal as the current conflict in the Balkans have occurred in the land of Medjugorje? This discussion leads to the conclusion that Medjugorje itself symbolizes a growing rupture between Eastern and Western culture.

We would like to thank Texas A&M University for travel grants that enabled the coauthors of this book to collaborate. In addition, we are grateful to Ben Crouch, Chris Rojek, Barry Smart, Barry Glassner, Deena and Michael Weinstein, Michael Kaern, Noel Parsons, and David Riesman for engaging us in discussions that pertain to this project. Of course, the coauthors are solely responsible for the final argument that is put forth here. Meštrović acknowledges the permission of the *World and I* magazine to elaborate upon an article entitled "Habits of the Heart: Eastern Europe and the Possibility of Democracy," vol. 6, no. 3 (March 1991): 574–93.

The frontispiece of this book features "Mother Meditating" by the Croatian-born sculptor Ivan Meštrović (1883–1962). It was sculpted in marble in 1930 and can still be found in the Meštrović Gallery in Zagreb. We chose it to highlight, in a concrete and immediate way, several aspects of the argument that follows in this book: the theme of the mother-centered culture, the controversial role of Ivan Meštrović and other Croatian intellectuals in the formation of Yugoslavia, and the fact that Ivan Meštrović was born and raised in the same Dinaric culture that we criticize as being mostly responsible for the current, tragic war in the Balkans. The obvious point we wish to make is that despite its negative aspects, the Balkan habits of the heart also have their beauty and dignity, as illustrated by this moving piece of art.

Habits of the Balkan Heart

1. The Collapse of Communism and Its Cultural Nemesis

When the Berlin Wall was torn down in November of 1989 and Communism allegedly began to die, the dominant response in Western Europe and the United States was euphoria. It was assumed by most commentators that capitalism and democracy had "won" the long war with socialism and totalitarianism.[1] A "golden age of capitalism" was predicted in the pages of the *Wall Street Journal*. Francis Fukuyama (1992) declared the "end of history," by which he meant the triumph of liberal democracy over nationalism, totalitarianism, and imperialism.[2] The extreme optimists predicted that the establishment of democratic and free-market institutions in Eastern Europe and the former USSR would take only a few years.[3] Even the typically cautious foreign affairs expert Zbigniew Brzezinski (1989) expressed the view that humanity was witnessing the end of the "grand failure" of Communism, which would eventually be replaced with freedom and democracy. Contrary to every premise of authentic sociology, most of these commentators forgot that democratic and free-market institutions are culture-specific artifacts peculiar to a specific time and place in Western history, not universally valid phenomena.

The two short years since the alleged death of Communism in Eastern Europe and the former USSR have not supported these naive, optimistic, and ideologically based hopes.[4] On the contrary, in 1991 a particularly savage war erupted in what used to be Yugoslavia. A coup was staged against Gorbachev in Moscow in August of 1991. The democratically elected leader of what used to be So-viet Georgia was ousted in a coup. Fighting also broke out in Ar-menia and Azerbaijan. Instead of the rule of law and the smoothly functioning federations that the West had sought, nationalism emerged as the most powerful social force in formerly Communist lands. The maps of Eastern Europe and the former USSR had to be changed as seemingly new, completely alien-sounding nations declared their independence, one after the other: Slovenia, Croatia, Macedonia, Bosnia, Ukraine, Tadzhikistan, Armenia, Kirghizia, Byelorussia, and Kazakhstan, among many others. Even Russia began to unravel as its minorities began to rebel against centralized rule from Moscow.

The fundamental sociological assumption that all these pre-viously submerged nations had their own cultures and their own "habits of the heart" that might be different from Western habits of the heart was ignored by politicians, the media, and most commen-tators—even many contemporary sociologists. In general, the West responded to the rapid but unexpected changes with alarm and paralysis, because according to Western cultural standards, the new-ly emerging nationalism was denigrated to the status of dangerous "tribalism."[5] And all tribalism is assumed to threaten the modernist order. Thus, pro-Communist Serbia had already taken over most of democratic Croatia's territory before Germany could convince the rest of the European Community in January of 1992 to recognize Croatia's right to democratic self-determination. What would hap-pen to all those nuclear weapons in the former USSR? Would the commonwealth hold, or would the situation in the former Soviet Union deteriorate into a civil war that was foreshadowed by the former Yugoslavs, as Gorbachev had warned?

Following David Riesman (1964), one might characterize the Western response to events in post-Communist lands as exhibiting an attitude of "provincial cosmopolitanism." The modern West sees only cosmopolitanism because that is the cultural basis of its exis-tence, and it is blind to other social forces, particularly national-ism. Nationalism is a key aspect of tradition and history, and according to Fukuyama and other modernists, history came to an end. But this parochial cosmopolitanism makes the West seem provincial, not cosmopolitan, when compared with the realities of the post-Communist world. These realities include phenomena that are on the other end of the spectrum of cosmopolitanism, namely, brutality, nationalism, authoritarianism, and a sort of compulsion to repeat old, Communist evils.

We shall argue that the actual course of events that followed the alleged death of Communism had been predicted by the sociologist Dinko Tomašić, who wrote two books on Yugoslav and Soviet social character in 1948 and 1953 respectively, among other publications.[6] By using the once-standard sociological term "social character," Tomašić was able to trace the antecedents of Communism to the autocratic "habits of the heart" that had preceded it. By extrapolation, he was able to predict that without a self-conscious change in social character, the eventual collapse of Communism would not signal its actual death, as Brzezinski (1989) and others thought, but merely its metamorphosis into a new form of authoritarianism. The obvious but neglected point is that contrary to the West's tradition, which includes the Renaissance, the Reformation, the American Revolution, and the French Revolution, among many other cultural events that point in the direction of increasing respect for human rights, Eastern European and former Soviet habits of the heart flow from autocratic principles found in Byzantium.

In revivifying Tomašić and the sociological tradition upon which he drew, we do not mean to imply conclusions that a hasty reader might draw from reading only up to this point and not going further. Not all the cultural habits of the heart in Eastern Europe and the former Soviet Union are autocratic. In fact, the more peaceable and democratic traditions are the ones that need to be nurtured if the desired, democratic outcome is to be achieved in post-Communist lands. The more important point is that the West is naive to assume that the autocratic traditions have been extinguished simply because the mostly former Communist political leaders in Eastern Europe and what used to be the Soviet Union suddenly jumped on the democratic bandwagon. Our analysis is not meant to lead to further paralysis or pessimism but to act as a sobering and realistic explanation of developments that are understandable from the perspective that shall be taken here, yet are bewildering from the hyperoptimistic and ethnocentric perspective that has dominated public analysis of post-Communism up to now.

Nor do we wish to engage in an ideological glorification of the democratic principles enshrined by many Western nations. For the sake of objectivity, we point to Spengler, Toynbee, Sorokin, Ortega, and other cynical, pessimistic analysts of Western culture, who have regarded publicly espoused democratic principles as a cover for decadence, cultural decay, mass society, and even Western forms of totalitarianism.[7] We know that the notion of democracy is extremely problematic at the present time, even if a better alternative does not exist on the cultural horizon. Nevertheless, the aim in this book is to focus on the prospects for democracy in post-Communist nations, not the future of democracy in the West.

In the remainder of this chapter, we flesh out the meaning and use of the key terms "habits of the heart" and "social character," from Alexis de Tocqueville's classic *Democracy in America* (1845) through Thorstein Veblen (1899), David Riesman (1950), and, most recently, Bellah et al. (1985). Next, we lay the groundwork for examining what is required culturally for the reconstruction of post-Communist, Balkan societies. In chapter 3, we take up Tomašić's analysis of Slavic social character and try to demonstrate its relevance to current events in the Balkans. Chapter 4 continues the cultural analysis by reviewing Veblen's and Spengler's cultural analyses of the roots of World War I. Because no analysis is complete if it examines only the destructive aspects of a culture, in chapter 5 we touch briefly on the benign, peaceable aspects and how these relate to the rise and fall of Communism. We conclude in chapter 6 by exploring the question whether Communism really "died," as claimed by Brzezinski and others, and what a meaningful reply to this question might be like in the light of our cultural analysis.

The Alternatives to Hegel and Marx

The overall focus of the present book is on the role of the social character—the "habits of the heart" and "collective consciousness"—of the formerly Communist nations in Eastern Europe and what used to be the Soviet Union. How do these relate to the seemingly new, Slavic experiment in democracy? It seems natural to want to ask these questions in the aftermath of the fall of Communism in the present fin de siècle, yet these questions touch on vast controversies, and the supposed end of Communism has occurred at about the same time that the postmodernists are writing about the end of history, and sociologists are worried about the end of their profession. Sociology was established as a respectable discipline and separated from its mother, philosophy, in the turn of the previous century, an era that was, in many ways, as turbulent as ours is today (see Meštrović 1991). Then, as now, intellectuals as well as laypersons debated the future of socialism, Communism, feminism, nationalism, human rights, and capitalism. Whereas the previous fin de siècle bore the signature of Schopenhauer, Nietzsche, and other philosophers who made the classic argument that the heart or will was more important than the mind in analyzing the world, the present fin de siècle is under the influence of the positivistic assumption that the mind can and should rule the heart.

Herein lies one of the most important lacunae in the contemporary discussions of the philosophical origins of these debates. Fukuyama (1992) draws primarily on Hegel and Marx to make his argument for the steady progress of liberal democracy. But he does not even mention Hegel's most vocal competitor and critic, Arthur Schopenhauer, who argued that nature offers us the spectacle of chaos, not progress. Moreover, Fukuyama seems almost completely unaware that in drawing on Hegel and Marx, as well as in promoting the concept of the end of history, he is repeating the arguments of the Bolsheviks. Our point is that an objective appraisal of the

Enlightenment-based theories of Hegel and Marx can be made only by contrasting them with opposing points of view. But these opposing points of view, which stress the primacy of the will over the mind (the latter which the Enlightenment has enshrined), tend to be neglected in modern times as well as in modern sociology. Without these philosophical distinctions, it is difficult to make sense of the dramatic political changes that have been occurring in our fin de siècle. Zbigniew Brzezinski (1989) has declared the death of Communism, but the Marxists are more determined than ever to prove that Soviet Communism was not genuine Marxism and that in the long run, Marx will be proved right. The postmodernists, from Lyotard to Baudrillard, have argued that history has ended and that one should rebel at the oppressive narratives from the Enlightenment. Yet they are countered by Habermas, Giddens, and other intellectual heirs to Talcott Parsons who seek to complete the Enlightenment project, despite Horkheimer and Adorno's *Dialectic of Enlightenment* (1972). Fukuyama also uses the concept "end of history" but, unlike the postmodernists, seems to put his hopes in the Enlightenment.

Or consider Zygmunt Bauman's (1992) elaboration on the theme that the collapse of Communism is a symptom of postmodernity.[8] He depicts the Communist dream of the perfect society as a manifestation of the *modernist* experiment in social engineering. If that is true, then the people who celebrate the collapse of Communism "celebrate more than that without always knowing it. They celebrate the end of modernity actually, because what collapsed was the most decisive attempt to make modernity work; and it failed" (1992:222). For the sake of argument, let us assume that Bauman is correct. In that case, efforts to export democracy and free-market institutions to post-Communist nations are an unwitting effort to replace a dead with a dying system of modernity. In order to avoid this unwelcome conclusion, Bauman depicts modernity on this side of the former Iron Curtain in benign terms, as "modernity emancipated from false consciousness" (p. 188) that leads to freedom and choice, which will avoid the cruel fate of the apparently "bad" version of modernity that took root in Communist nations. This is a self-serving argument that perpetuates the old ideology, and it is not logical. The logical alternatives to Bauman's arguments are that (1) the capitalist version of modernity will also collapse, (2) capitalism is not really a modern doctrine, or (3) what passes for capitalist modernity is a mixture of modern and nonmodern elements.

Missing in all of these highly abstract, jargon-filled accounts of dramatic endings is the notion of culture. Modernity, postmodernity, history, and Communism are depicted as reified, self-begotten, a priori categories, floating through history as if they were clouds. For example, it does not seem to have occurred to Brzezinski that an authoritarian mind-set might have preceded Communism and that it might fester secretly beneath the surface victory of democracy.[9] Bauman does not consider that even if Communism is a modernist doctrine, it failed to modernize or change dramatically the medieval mind-set of the people it ruled. Almost as soon as Communism fell in 1989, the post-Communist nations *stepped back into history* and did not make appreciable strides in becoming like the West. Nationalism, ethnocentrism, fundamentalism, Balkanization, and other phenomena that Fukuyama had declared dead returned with a vengeance. Caught almost completely off guard, the West responded with denial and paralysis.

Finally, and despite the fact that Talcott Parsons (1937) had eclipsed completely the pessimistic sociology of Pitirim Sorokin (1957), the Russian-born sociologist who had hired him at Harvard University, there is the legacy left over from the previous fin de siècle, as refracted in the works of Sorokin (1948), Toynbee (1962), and Spengler (1926), that likens the current phase of Western civilization to Rome in its last, dying stages: unspiritual, unphilosophical, brutal, commercialized, egoistic, and therefore profoundly immoral.[10] These theorists must be admitted into any discussion of the future of post-Communism if that discussion shall be objective and evenhanded.

What little is clear in this crowded discussion is that, in

Spengler's (1926:32) words, the transition from culture (which is based on the soul or the heart) to civilization[11] (which is the domain of the intellect) occurred in the Western world in the nineteenth century.[12] Spengler's argument is corroborated by scores of writers who noted something similar, even if they used only slightly different terminology. Thus, Ferdinand Tönnies (1887) documented the change from *Gemeinschaft*, or community based on the mother-child archetype, to *Gesellschaft*, or society based on commerce. Schopenhauer, Simmel, Nietzsche, and other fin-de-siècle intellectuals also noted the transition from culture based on sentiments, sympathy, and feelings (or the heart) to society or civilization based on utilitarian principles, commercialism, and egoism. Veblen (1899) even distinguished between "habits of the heart," which he applied to a mythical, matriarchal culture (based on Bachofen) in the remote past, and "habits of the mind," or thought, which he used to explain modern forms of barbarism. It is a safe assertion that sociology was born about a century ago in Western Europe as humanity began to feel the consequences of this dramatic shift in the cultural center of gravity. We believe that the drama of Communism's apparent collapse in our turn of the century begs for a genuinely sociological (i.e., cultural) explanation and offers an important opportunity for sociology to renew its relevance. This is what we shall attempt here, albeit in a preliminary fashion, as we can present little more than a thumbnail sketch of what such an application of sociological theory should be like.

The Concepts of Social Character and Habits of the Heart

One might conclude hastily and incorrectly that there is something idiosyncratic and perhaps even archaic in our reliance on the concepts "habits of the heart" and "social character." After all, most contemporary sociologists do not use these terms, and the sociological profession is not in the forefront of popularity, public debate, or high enrollments today compared to a century ago, when it was established in Europe. Actually, however, several distinguished sociologists have followed Alexis de Tocqueville's line of reasoning in *Democracy in America* (1845) that each nation's experiment in democracy must be unique to some extent because it is based on what he called the habits of the heart of a people—even though he also claimed that some sort of democracy is the inevitable endpoint for all humanity as it evolves. Tocqueville was a French social critic and philosopher who traveled widely across the United States in the 1830s in order to assess, compare, and contrast the American with the French experiments in democracy. His *Democracy in America* is widely regarded as a classic but, oddly enough, is rarely cited in current debates on the possibility of democracy in Eastern Europe and the former USSR.[13]

Emile Durkheim (1893), Thorstein Veblen (1899), Oswald Spengler (1926), Pitirim Sorokin (1948), David Riesman (1950), Arnold Toynbee (1962), Robert N. Bellah et al. (1985), and Erich Fromm (1955), among others, have followed in the wake of these intriguing assertions made by Tocqueville to some extent. In fact, Bellah et al. took the title of their best-selling analysis of American social character, *Habits of the Heart*, directly from Tocqueville. We find it interesting that in the preface to their popular book, they claim that their research is neither psychological nor sociological but cultural (Bellah et al. 1985:ix). The study of culture has been neglected in the twentieth century by a primarily positivistic social science.

Nevertheless, in addition to Bellah and his colleagues, the other authors we have listed above have referred to Tocqueville's "habits of the heart" as social character, culture, collective representations, or other equivalents. Essentially, they agree with de Tocqueville that (1) democracy in general is the eventual, "final" stage of human development, (2) there exist many paths to democracy and many varieties of it, and (3) each people's virtues that made democracy possible are also related to each people's vices. For example, the so-called high priest of postmodernism, Jean Baudrillard, observes in his own *America* (1986) that Tocqueville contrasted the "good" America of freedom, democracy, and high regard for the individual with the "bad" America that institutionalized slavery and exterminated the Indians. Other contemporary writers focus on the American vices of anomie, narcissism, and superficiality as they continue to coexist with moral ideals of democracy that most of the modern, Western world seems to applaud (see Bloom 1987, Lasch 1991, Riesman 1980a).

Emile Durkheim might be regarded as the only genuine founding father of sociology, not just because he was the first philosopher to be appointed to a chair in sociology, but also because he drew on Tocqueville to posit a "collective consciousness" that is distinct from an individual's consciousness. In other words, both Tocqueville and Durkheim posit that social character or collective consciousness is a group property that influences individuals and that society is something quite distinct from the sum of its parts. Without this fundamental assumption, sociology loses its raison d'être and is reduced to psychology or, worse, idle speculation.

Similarly, Thorstein Veblen was widely regarded as the greatest American sociologist of the previous turn of the century—even though he, too, came to sociology via philosophy and economics—because of his reliance on the concept of habit. He felt that phenomena that range from barbarism to parenting skills are not innate or learned in a behaviorist, stimulus-response fashion but become "second nature" by virtue of being habits. Habits are notoriously difficult to learn as well as unlearn, and once they are established, they feel like instincts. Erich Fromm, too, referred to cultural habits as substitutes for instinct, that is, seemingly automatic ways of perceiving and behaving that are taken for granted in a given cultural group. All of these theorists deny that a universal, rational explanation for any human phenomenon exists, for the simple reason that habits are culture specific.

David Riesman is an important conduit for the preservation of the concepts "habits of the heart" and "social character" in twentieth-century American sociology. His own best seller *The Lonely Crowd* is subtitled, "An Exploration of American Social Character." Riesman has written on Tocqueville and Veblen, both of whom influenced him, and cites Erich Fromm as an important mentor. Riesman is also cited by Bellah as an influence upon *Habits of the Heart*. In general, Riesman's relevance to our discussion may be summarized as follows: With regard to Tocqueville, Riesman exposes Tocqueville's importance as a sort of anthropologist or ethnographer, Tocqueville's ambivalence toward America as a key to the future, and the importance of this question: What remains of Tocqueville's America when one takes into account industrialization, urbanization, and immigration?[14]

With regard to Freud, Riesman is important in pointing to Freud's contributions to the study of national character. The psychoanalytic applications to the notion of social or national character also show up in some works by the critical theorists of the Frankfurt School, whose members include Erich Fromm, Theodor Adorno, Max Horkheimer, and Herbert Marcuse. The critical theorists came up with the notion of authoritarian personality as a manifestation of social character in an effort to explain the rise of German fascism. Although most contemporary sociologists refer to *The Authoritarian Personality* in pejorative terms, as if it were completely discredited,[15] we take its starting premises very seriously. We shall argue that an authoritarian social character exists in Eastern Europe and the former Soviet Union as well and that its consequences might be similar to those that followed from German authoritarianism.

In sum, Riesman exposes the importance of the questions that are first found in Tocqueville's writings and that have reverberated in many important works since then: What is American about America? Have Americans changed since Tocqueville's time? If so, in what directions may they be going? What differences within America matter most? What is America's role in a world setting? How shall one assess values and directions in the context of the notion of social character? We believe that these continue to be extremely important questions for Americans in a post-Communist setting. We intend to add, however, that the same questions that may be asked concerning American social character need to be asked of Eastern European and former Soviet social characters. Moreover, each of these questions needs to be asked with an eye toward America's role in foreign affairs, not the provincial perspective of understanding American social character for its own sake.

What about democracy in Eastern Europe and what used to be the Soviet Union? What is their social character, their "habits of the heart"? In other words, what is Croatian about the Croatians, and Serbian about the Serbians, and so on for the many nationalities that make up the mosaic of what used to pass for Eastern Europe and the Soviet Union? How have they changed since the Bolshevik Revolution—or have they? In what direction are they going? What similarities among them matter most? What is their role in the earth-shaking changes that are occurring today? Shall they follow passively in the wake of America's revolutionary role as depicted by Toynbee (1962) or in the wake of the European Community or of their own national character? How shall following the course set by their nationalist agendas ever result in cosmopolitanism and world unity? To begin to answer these and related questions, one needs to understand what is significant in the philosophical, methodological, and sociological dimensions to the concept "habits of the heart."

What Are Habits of the Heart?

The phrase "habits of the heart" and the focus on habits in general by William James, Veblen, Weber, Durkheim, Simmel, and other founding fathers of sociology was replaced, beginning in the 1920s, with a vocabulary of rational social action, rational choice theory, and other derivatives of positivism. The original study of culture as a manifestation of collective consciousness that was popular in the previous fin de siècle was replaced with an approach to society as a social system devoid of culture that could be studied using methods established by natural sciences. Contemporary sociology has grudgingly conceded the importance of culture to some extent with the advent of the postmodernist movement, but even then, postmodernism thoroughly permeated philosophy, literature, the arts, and architecture before it was admitted into sociological discourse (Rosenau 1992). In sum, it seems that contemporary sociologists are suspicious of the concept "social character" and of its original precursor, Tocqueville's "habits of the heart." When confronted with these concepts, many sociologists ask, in a positivistic vein, How do you operationalize social character? How do you test the hypothesis that social character "causes" behavior?

Our reply to these questions shall be necessarily brief, but to the point. We do not intend to operationalize the notions of social character or habits of the heart, nor do we intend to "test" hypotheses. In the first place, the terms "habits of the heart" and their equivalents were invented in the fin-de-siècle interregnum between Comte's positivism and the positivism of the 1920s, in a time and place that emphasized the *explanation* of social phenomena on the basis of theory. Theory was used as a context for the *interpretation* of social reality, not as the basis for the generation of hypotheses to be falsified (see also Bellah et al. 1985). One should not forget that the founding fathers of sociology were philosophers by training, not natural scientists engaged in hypothesis testing.

Second, the positivistic program cannot give a final account or explanation of any phenomenon because all its findings are assumed to be contingent and subject to being proven false. A genuine positivist believes that nothing can be proved to be true but that everything can be proved false. Such assumptions are of little practical use to politicians or even intelligent laypersons who seek to understand, as we do, what is occurring in post-Communist lands, and what the future might hold in store.

Third, it could very well be the case, as argued by postmodernists, that positivistic sociology is an exercise in Eurocentric ethnocentrism, an oppressive grand narrative that is irrelevant to cultures that are not cut from the cloth of Western Enlightenment. We seek to understand a region of the world that is still mysterious to contemporary Westerners.

Finally, we follow Spengler's (1926) methodological critique of positivism as applied to history and the rest of the social sciences. The social sciences are not like the natural sciences, because they involve human actors embedded in living cultures that vary tremendously in time and space. The laws of gravity are invariant, but the same cannot be said of the "laws" of democratic development or of any other cultural phenomenon. This does not necessarily mean that science should be subsumed under culture (as some have interpreted Spengler to imply),[16] or that cultural analysis is unscientific. Rather, we hark back to the original inspiration for sociology at the turn of the previous century and the belief that the methods to be followed in cultural analysis are different from those of the natural sciences. The primary differences lie in the focus on the notion of habit, induction as opposed to deduction, and the use of theory to illuminate the meaning of "social facts" (from Durkheim) in opposition to the belief that facts speak for themselves.

Consider, for example, Spengler's (1926:108) typically fin-de-siècle understanding of the concept "habit," with all of the methodological implications discussed above:

> We may apply this useful notion of "habit" in our physiognomic of the grand organisms and speak of the habit of the Indian, Egyptian or Classical Culture, history or spirituality. Some vague inkling of it has always, for that matter, underlain the notion of *style*, and we shall not be forcing but merely clearing and deepening that word if we speak of the religious, intellectual, political, social or economic style of a Culture. This "habit" of existence in space, which covers in the case of the individual man action and thought and conduct and disposition, embraces in the case of whole Cultures the totality of life-expressions of the higher order. . . . To the "habit" of a group belong, further, its definite *life-duration* and its definite tempo of development. Both of these are properties which we must not fail to take into account in a historical theory of structure.

In contradistinction to Fukuyama and the modernists who posit the existence of one, universal history, Spengler claims that there exist as many histories as there are cultures. Fukuyama's viewpoint might be termed ethnocentric, even if Spengler's claim runs into the problem of how one should evaluate so many histories and cultures. Our purpose is to expand the discussion, not resolve these difficulties at this point.

Similarly, William James's ([1890] 1950:169) famous essay on habit can scarcely be improved and still seems fresh and relevant to contemporary, modern times.

> Habit is thus the enormous fly-wheel of society, its most precious conservative agent. It alone is what keeps us all within the bounds of ordinance and saves the children of fortune from the envious uprisings of the poor. It alone prevents the hardest and most repulsive walks of life from being deserted by those brought up to tread therein. It keeps the fisherman and the deck-hand at sea through the winter; it holds the miner in his darkness and nails the countryman to his log-cabin and his lonely farm through all the months of snow; it protects us from invasion by the natives of the desert and the frozen zone. It dooms us all to fight out the battle of life upon the lines of our nurture or our early choices and to make the best of a pursuit that disagrees, because there is no other for which we are fitted and it is too late to begin again. It keeps different social strata from mixing. Already at the age of twenty-five you see the professional mannerism settling down on the young commercial traveler, on the young doctor, on the young minister, on the young counsellor-at-law. You see the little lines of cleavage running through the character, the tricks of thought, the prejudices, the ways of the "shop," in a word, from which the man can by-and-by no more escape than his coat-sleeve can suddenly fall into a new set of folds. On the whole, it is best he should not escape. It is well for the world that in most of us, by the age of thirty, the character has set like plaster and will never soften again.

William James reminds us that without the force of habit, anarchy and chaos would rule the social world. The modernists and postmodernists who write of the eradication of traditional habits really overstate their case. Without the conservative force of habits, even the modernist project, the Enlightenment, and the principles of liberal democracy could not exist, for these phenomena, like all others, are maintained by habits and are not calculated rationally and anew with each passing event.

The Fall of Communism and Its Aftermath

We contend that the original conceptual vocabulary of sociology from the previous fin de siècle serves as a more adequate basis for analyzing and comprehending contemporary heart-over-mind (i.e., genuinely irrational) post-Communist manifestations. In the absence of a liberal tradition that harks back to the Enlightenment philosophers in the West, the vacuum left in post-Communist Slavic nations has been filled by the only cultural traditions that survived Communism: nationalism, religion, the family, and other centripetal forces that bespeak the power of habits of the heart. The use of mind-over-heart conceptual vocabulary by the West to perceive heart-over-mind phenomena in the USSR and Eastern Europe seems incongruous and is a manifestation of provincial cosmopolitanism.

The present book is not intended to be more than a first step or outline in the cultural study of the habits of the heart that were important before, during, and following the fall of Communism in Eastern Europe and what used to be the Soviet Union. It is intended to serve as the basis for further discussion and elaboration and for the eventual application of qualitative research methods in Eastern Europe and the former USSR. Despite the lack of such empirical, cultural studies at the present time, the problem at hand is intellectually manageable. Dinko Tomašić has already addressed the essential problem that concerns us in his *Personality and Culture in Eastern European Politics* (1948b) and *The Impact of Russian Culture on Soviet Communism* (1953). He and other Slavic authors writing in this vein use Yugoslavia as the vehicle for discussion,[17] even though they make it clear that their intentions are to discuss the commonalties that pertain to Slavic culture in all of Eastern Europe, including portions of Russia. We agree with Tomašić and other students of Slavic culture in this regard, although notable differences among various Slavic nations exist. The problem is not essentially different from Tocqueville's wide-ranging discussion of American habits of the heart, despite his admission that these habits vary regionally to some extent.

In other words, at the present time, one may regard Dinko Tomašić as a sort of precursor to an eventual Tocqueville of the Slavs. Tocqueville might never have launched his influential study of American social character had he worried excessively about defining and distinguishing Americans from non-Americans, or the ways in which southerners were distinct from Yankees—even though these were very important concerns for him, as we shall see. Still, he managed to write his *Democracy in America*. Similarly, we admit that scholars debate questions pertaining to Slavic origins and identity, but these issues are not directly relevant to our concerns. One can make careful generalizations about American as well as Slavic social character, as long as one admits that variations in social character do exist. We make this admission from the outset. We shall focus on what used to be Yugoslavia as the vehicle for discussion in the hope that some of our analysis shall be relevant to other, neighboring cultures, but with the prudent caution that important differences exist. In any case, Tomašić's books are the closest equivalent to *Democracy in America* in a Slavic context, and for this reason we shall analyze Tomašić's findings, using them as a springboard for further discussion.

Tomašić was a Croatian sociologist steeped in Tocqueville, Veblen, Durkheim, and the fin-de-siècle tradition of sociology. He emigrated eventually to the United States and settled in the sociology department at Indiana University. It is interesting that his books were banned by Tito in Yugoslavia. As of this writing, they are available in English but not in any of the Slavic languages. His central claim—that Communism is built upon a "bad" side to the Slavic social character that preceded Marxism—explains how and why Marxism took root and eventually died in Slavic lands (although his writings suggest that it may resurrect itself in a new form). Although Tomašić remained obscure during the era of the Cold War, in which hardly anyone took seriously the possibility that Communism might collapse of its own accord, the fall of Communism in the end of the present century demands that his claims be taken seriously.

A New Way of Conceptualizing the Fall of Communism

There is little doubt that the fall of Communism in Eastern Europe and the USSR in recent years is one of the most significant events of the twentieth century. Western scholarly and popular presses, however, have been reluctant to publish anything on the subject that is not merely descriptive or ideological. The ideological statements usually involve diatribes against Marxism or accolades for Western capitalism and clichés about the will of the people. For example, Brucan (1989, 1990) makes a Marxist argument for the demise of Marxism, namely, that the emergence of a new class structure in the Soviet Union made glasnost possible. Goldfarb (1989) overestimates "people power" in the Polish Solidarity movement without accounting for anti-Semitic and other negative aspects of the "will of the people." Moreover, he never explains the origins of a democratic movement within Communist Poland and accepts its rise as if it were a mushroom that springs up in a dark forest. Muravchick (1991) assumes that Western democracy can be exported to the post-Communist lands. Missing in the already vast and constantly growing literature on the fall of Communism is a non-Marxist, nonideological, *theoretically* informed conceptual apparatus for apprehending the dramatic changes that have occurred among the Slavs.

This is what we shall attempt in the present work. We hold no allegiance to either Marxist or neoconservative programs. Our position is that of a detached observer; it is sociological in the sense of authentic, cultural sociology of a century ago. We shall rely on two of the most basic concepts in the sociological vocabulary—social character and habits of the heart—in order to analyze dispassionately the antecedents, nature, and consequences of the fall of Communism in the Balkans, as well as the subsequent rebirth of history.[18] To be sure, we hope that the post-Communist lands will eventually discover democracy, but we do not believe that theirs will be the sorts of democracy that are assumed as a matter of course in the West. Rather, each post-Communist nation will fit democracy to its unique history and culture.

Moreover, our analysis may be regarded as sociological in the context of the cultural sociological trajectory that we have already sketched from Tocqueville to Riesman and Bellah. We do not identify with the positivistic bias of contemporary sociology. In the first place, the sociological profession has been tardy in responding to the fall of Communism. For example, during the annual meetings of the American Sociological Association held in 1991 in Cincinnati, Ohio, only 2 out of 323 sessions were devoted to Eastern Europe and the USSR. The relatively few sociologists who are doing research among the Slavs tend to employ positivistic methods, including surveys and questionnaires. Such an approach assumes that social forces are universal—that the same forces pertaining to social mobility, for example, operate in Oklahoma as well as the Ukraine. Yet, this positivistic assumption has been challenged by contemporary philosophers of science as well as postmodernists. Moreover, if it were true, one could not explain why travelers from Oklahoma to the Ukraine experience widespread cultural differences. Even if it is somewhat true that in the West, modernity tends to eradicate regional differences through assimilation (cf. Bauman 1991)—so that Oklahoma is not vastly different from Florida—one must concede that the same is not true for Slavic culture. For example, Croats perceive themselves to be vastly different from Serbs, even though, by most "objective" criteria, they seem to share what appears to Westerners to be the same ethnic identity. Even Max Weber (1958b:172) noted that national identity is a matter of cultural values, not objective criteria, and specifically cited the differences between the Croats and Serbs as illustration.

Eastern European presses and media are saturated with opinions, theories, and even guesses as to the future of their newfound experiment in democracy that run the gamut from success at emulating the West to the possibility of Balkanization, chaos, and a return to totalitarianism.[19] Westerners seems to fear that since the events and surface movements in Eastern Europe appear to be changing extremely rapidly, any commitment to a point of view might be proved to be wrong at a later time. Nevertheless, the guiding premise in the West seems to be the ideological one, that through the "right" social engineering, societies based on the free-market and democratic principles shall be established in formerly Communist lands (see Harwood 1991). The other, darker possibilities are dismissed as pessimism. This response by the West is in keeping with Western culture's own optimistic habits of the heart and faith in unequivocal, linear progress, but it is not necessarily realistic. As illustration, consider the following portion of a "letter from the publisher" of the *Wall Street Journal*, Peter R. Kann, found in the edition of January 9, 1992:

> It began with a bang and ended with a whimper. From the bang of a sweeping American-led victory in the Persian Gulf to the whimper with which the Soviet Union expired, 1991 by any historic measure was an extraordinary year. . . . No year is perfect. Saddam still sits in Baghdad, Serbs shell Croats, Somalis slaughter each other and recession lingers here at home. But, with the collapse of communism and the toppling of all but a few despotic dominos, we are poised at the threshold of an era in which men and women everywhere can grasp the almost limitless potential inherent in free politics and free markets and in the scientific and technological advances they unleash. (p. A-13)

Still another dominant, collective response by Americans in particular involves what Robert N. Bellah (1967) called American civil religion. In developing this popular and controversial concept, Bellah relied on the Durkheimian (1912) idea that a "religion" can exist independently of bona fide churches as long as it involves representations of the sacred and the profane. In this sense, American civil religion involves the celebration of American holidays, ideals, and images of America as the bastion of democracy blessed by God.

There can be no doubt that American civil religion was revived significantly by the Reagan and Bush administrations before and during the fall of Communism. Many intellectuals and laypersons alike view the collapse of Communism as a victory of the American way of life. The United States is purported to have *won* the Cold War, and conservatives are proud of the fact that they refused peaceful coexistence with the "evil empire" that used to be the Soviet Union.

We have no quarrels with the American way of life per se, even though the Frankfurt School, informed as it was by Marxist thought, has been highly critical of some aspects of Americanism (in particular, its tendency toward "mass society").[20] We would focus on a potentially larger and more important issue. Even though Bellah made the concept of American civil religion famous, one has to assume, following Durkheim (1912), that every people has its civil religion. Furthermore, and as noted by Bellah, the celebration of national identity leads easily into ethnocentrism and imperialistic adventures of many sorts. Thus, it is of interest to the sociologist who wishes to maintain some degree of objectivity that in the present fin de siècle, the revival of civil religions seems more noisy than ever and has spilled over, in many cases, into intolerance of other people's civil religions. In other words, we do not wish to embark on the popular, ideological analysis of current events through the perspectives imposed by one's civil religion and ethnocentrism but to strive after a more objective appraisal that notes the opposing tendencies of cosmopolitanism versus particularism.

For example, Croatia's declaration of independence coincided with popular revivals of Croatian history, language, mythology, and other aspects of its culture. The former Square of the Republic in its capital city, as it was named by the Communists, was renamed after one of its heroes, Viceroy Jelačić. The Communists had neglected to destroy the huge, bronze statue of this viceroy, and it was found following the open and free elections that threw the Communists out of power in 1990. The statue was placed back in the square during a solemn ceremony that invoked what might be called Croatian civil religion. But at the same time, Croatia longs to join the cosmopolitan European community and common market. The conflict between particularism versus cosmopolitanism is well established in sociology and seems particularly applicable to current events in Eastern Europe and the former USSR.

Thus, we seek to move beyond the almost exclusive focus on American civil religion and America as the center of the post–World War II cultural universe, not because we fail to admire America (we do admire it), but for the sake of an objective appraisal of the future of post-Communism. Since World War II, European sociologists have been moving steadily away from the European fin-de-siècle tradition that begat sociology and have been emulating American social theorists. As illustration, consider the preoccupation of contemporary British sociologist Anthony Giddens with American functionalists and southern California ethnomethodologists (discussed in Bryant and Jary 1991), or even the claim of the French Marxist Jean Baudrillard (1986) that America is the dawning of the universe. We feel that this overreliance on American concepts has to lead to bias and ethnocentrism. In this book, we are moving back to the original, European sociological tradition in order to assess Eastern European and former Soviet, post-Communist changes in a more objective light. The heightened objectivity stems solely from a shift of perspectives, not from any metaphysical or essentialist reason.

Thus, we are not concerned with the American bias toward conservatism and penchant for "social order" made famous by Talcott Parsons, which leads to paralysis with regard to Eastern Europeans because of rapid change. Instead, and in keeping with Tocqueville's original intent, we suppose that one can search for stable, constant factors (what Durkheim referred to as social *facts* in opposition to *events*) in the culturally based habits of the heart of Eastern Europeans. For us, the important question then becomes: How do these habits of the heart relate to the democratic revolution in Eastern Europe and what used to be the USSR? The advantage of such a cultural approach is that it focuses on underlying, chronic, and persistent factors that cast the surface events into their proper context. It is possible to argue that beneath all the apparent transitions, there exist pockets of social character in the Balkans that are unsuited to democracy as it is practiced in the West, and that there exists a real danger of regression to previous, undemocratic forms of government.

Problematics in the East-West Dichotomy

On the basis of his review of the formation of political states in Eastern Europe from the Middle Ages to 1948, Tomašić concluded that "the origin of these states can be found in the personality traits of the [Slavic] predatory herdsmen and the military whose power-seeking traits have remained basically unchanged throughout the centuries" (1948b:115). If Tomašić is correct and the cultural approach to the future of post-Communism holds merit, one has to fear for the possibility that "all new Eastern European state formations which are organized along the same lines will undoubtedly share the fate of their predecessors" (p. 116).

In other words, Tomašić warns of the return or rebirth of history in the Balkans because neither the West nor the citizens of the Balkans really understand the reasons why this region of the world has earned its reputation as the cauldron of militarism and despotism in Europe. To repeat, we focus on Tomašić in order to highlight and contrast the assumptions in Fukuyama's end-of-history thesis.

Political cartoons in Yugoslavia, which liken the fall of Communism to an airline crash, inquire, "Can we find the voice recorder?" Modernists do not know how or why Communism took root in Eastern European culture rather than the bourgeois world, as predicted by Marx. But this is an important question, if one is to avoid the subsequent rise of another form of totalitarianism in this region. Marx in fact never took Yugoslavia or the Eastern Europeans seriously—he regarded these regions as barbaric and backward. Moreover, because Eastern Europe was dominated by nobility well into this century, it never developed the bourgeois mentality that is essential to explaining Western culture. Thus, *contemporary Eastern Europe finds itself in an identity crisis.* To what extent does it share the culture and fate of Western Europe and its gravitation toward the values of human rights and individualism, and to what extent have the Mongol, Turkish, and other Asian conquests left it with a distinct cultural heritage that might be termed autocratic?

But the West is no less ambivalent about the relationship of its Enlightenment-based culture to democracy and totalitarianism. In *Dialectic of the Enlightenment*, Horkheimer and Adorno (1972) address—but never resolve—the issue of how Western Enlightenment could have led to Hitler's totalitarianism and anti-Semitism. Most subsequent approaches to totalitarianism, especially the works by the Frankfurt School, have been refracted through Western and Enlightenment assumptions. The central aim in this book is to suggest that Eastern European totalitarianism may be fundamentally different in its origins, nature, and consequences from the issues exposed in *Dialectic of the Enlightenment* and other works by critical theorists. We do not wish to be dogmatic about the alternative explanation to be offered here. It is offered for further discussion and refinement.

An important point of clarification is in order before we proceed in this discussion. The adjective "Eastern" is used here not in a geographic sense but to denote a cultural outlook that is relatively antithetical to "Western," liberal ideals of what ought to constitute democracy. And the East-West dichotomy that is assumed in this discussion is meant to be apprehended as a continuum of cultural influences. Thus, "central" Europe, in a geographic sense, is perceived as a region that will have to sort out its East-West identity crisis and the various legacies of Austro-Hungarian versus Turkish and other Eastern influences. We would predict that Hungary, the former Czechoslovakia, Slovenia, and Croatia are more likely to enter the Western orbit of cultural values, unlike Romania, Bulgaria, Serbia, Montenegro, and other geographic regions that were more dominated by Eastern cultural values, especially the southern and eastern flanks of what used to be the Soviet Union (Kirghizia,

Tadzhikistan, Uzbekistan, Turkmenia, Azerbaijan, Armenia, Georgia, and Moldavia).

But having made this claim, we wish to add the caveat that our intent is to problematize the East-West distinction, not reify it, which will become clear as the discussion progresses. Up to this point, our intent has been merely to lay the groundwork for what follows.

2. The Fifth Yugoslavia and the New World Order

Until recently, Western analysts have tended to display a modernist, globalizing tendency to refer to one USSR, one Yugoslavia, one United States—even one world. A significant consequence of post-Communism has been the breakup not only of ideological empires like the USSR and Yugoslavia but of modernist and global thinking. It seems that suddenly, analysts are exposed to more differences than ever before with regard to the concepts that they took for granted.

For example, in his *Fourth Yugoslavia*, Slaven Letica (1989) summarizes the emergence of four separate Yugoslavias.

1. The First Yugoslavia was a monarchy that lasted from 1918 to 1934, erected following the liberation of Slavic kingdoms from the Turks (following the Balkan Wars).

2. The Second Yugoslavia lasted from 1939 to 1943 and saw Croatia embrace the Nazis in order to secure its independence from what it perceived to be Serbian domination in Yugoslavia. The rest of Yugoslavia fought with the Allies or against each other.

3. The Third Yugoslavia lasted from 1945 to 1974 as a Communist federation under the iron fist of Tito.

4. The Fourth Yugoslavia emerged in 1980, following Tito's death, and existed as a loose confederation until 1990, when Communism succumbed to democratic elections in

Croatia and Slovenia but survived elections in Serbia and Montenegro. As of 1991, the Fifth Yugoslavia emerged, consisting only of Serbia and Montenegro, following democratic elections in Macedonia, Vojvodina, Kosovo, and Bosnia-Hercegovina, all of which sought independence. A quick glance over the previous century, and further back, suggests that history was never quieted or eliminated in favor of modernist, assimilatory forces in the Balkans. Instead, and contrary to Fukuyama's thesis, contemporary humanity is witnessing a rebirth of history, a repetition of major cultural themes and processes from the previous fin de siècle and beyond. The people in what used to be Yugoslavia are caught in an identity crisis as to whether they are a part of Western or Eastern civilization. In this regard, Yugoslavia serves as a laboratory for the interplay of forces that will either preserve or splinter further the former USSR and the rest of Eastern Europe. This is because the dividing line between East and West runs roughly along the present-day border between Croatia and Serbia, which is known as the Krajina region. This is the region in which the fiercest fighting occurred in the war of 1991, as well as previous Balkan wars. Roughly the same border was established by the Roman emperor Diocletian (whose palace still stands in Split, Croatia) to divide the Western from the Eastern Roman empires. The Latin alphabet and Roman Catholicism were retained in Croatia and Slovenia, whereas the Cyrillic alphabet and Eastern Orthodox churches dominated Serbia and the other Eastern regions. Following the Battle of Kosovo in 1389, in which the South Slavs lost to the Turks, the eastern and southern portions of what came to be Yugoslavia were under Muslim and Ottoman cultural influence until 1912. By contrast, Croatia and Slovenia were part of the Austro-Hungarian empire from the eighteenth century up to World War I. The dividing line between the Hapsburg and Ottoman empires was similar to that of the Western and Eastern empires, as well as present-day Croatia and Slovenia versus the rest of former

Yugoslavia. The result is a sharp contrast in societal and cultural structures that helps to explain Yugoslav history, as well as its future.

For example, following the collapse of Communism in 1989, Croatia and Slovenia expressed publicly their eagerness to pursue the Western orbit of cultural values, even though neither republic had experienced the Reformation or the Renaissance. The Catholic church had maintained a universalist cultural base that is still medieval in many ways but is nevertheless recognizably Western. Thus, Croatia and Slovenia led the anti-Communist rebellion in 1989, voted for democracy, tend to favor pluralism, want to join the European Community, seek free-market institutions, and declared their independence from a Serbian-dominated federal government that emanates from Belgrade.

By contrast, Serbia and Montenegro tend in the direction of an Eastern orbit of cultural values. They typically have had close ties with Russia and are neo-Communist, following free elections in which democracy was rejected. Orthodox or Muslim in their religious orientation, they seek a pyramidal power structure and are militaristic. For example, Serbia and Montenegro, which had already dominated over 70 percent of the officer corps in the Yugoslav army, pulled the entire Yugoslav army (which is the third largest in Europe) into the defense of what was left of Yugoslavia, namely, Serbia and Montenegro. Since 1981, the Serbian government has been accused of perpetuating human rights abuses against the minority in Kosovo.[1]

The rest of the former Yugoslav republics are ethnically more heterogeneous and were less decisive in deciding their cultural identity along the ideal types described above. We would predict, however, that a similar identity crisis will eventually afflict all of them. For example, Bosnia-Hercegovina consists of Croats, Serbs, and Muslims and has become the fiercest theater of fighting in the Balkans.

The West in general and the United States in particular misread completely the cultural and historical roots of the post-Communist conflicts in the Balkans. The West tried to preserve an artificial Yugoslavia for purely modernist reasons: to maintain the status quo; to promote assimilatory, federalist, and centrifugal social forces that would lead to the fusion of smaller states into larger ones; and to contain "tribalism" and nationalism. There emerged even some evidence implicating Deputy Secretary of State Lawrence Eagleburger as having financial interests in Serbia that prevented him from acting fairly on behalf of the United States in the Balkans (Glynn 1992). But in the end, history won over modernist forces in the Balkans. Western Europe finally admitted this fact and recognized the independence of Croatia and Slovenia on January 15, 1992. But the United States continued to refuse to go along with its friends and allies well into March 1992. It clung stubbornly to the end-of-history thesis, despite all evidence to the contrary.

The Croatians and Slovenes thus looked to America as if it were the North Star that would guide them to democracy and the free market. This is a typically inner-directed reaction, according to David Riesman (1950), who uses the metaphor of wishing upon a distant star to capture the inner-directed type of person's longing for a remote but permanent value. According to Riesman, the shift to other-directedness in America and Western Europe revealed an entire galaxy of stars (values). Now, with the Milky Way looming before the human actor, it seems impossible to choose one value, position, or even country over another. Although America may shine brightly in the Slavic sky, most Americans cannot make out the differences among the many Slavic republics and nations clamoring to be heard and recognized. How many Americans knew the differences among Croatia, Slovenia, Serbia, and other Slavic nations when war broke out in 1991? Our point is that this lack of knowledge stems not only from American unfamiliarity with geography and history but, in keeping with Riesman's (1950) study, from American social character. Hypermodernity makes it exceedingly difficult to take a stand, to choose a value. The one value that is left is the most basic one, self-interest, which degenerates easily into old-fashioned narcissism and indifference.

The Two Americas and the Two Faces of the Balkans

Tocqueville's *Democracy in America* (1845) has been read typically as a sociological classic that laid the groundwork for contemporary studies of American social character, from Riesman (1950) to Bellah et al. (1985). Such studies have proven to be fruitful ways to gain inspiration from Tocqueville in a modernist, assimilatory era that has sought equality in a melting-pot context. Tocqueville, however, may have been misread when one considers the present, historical context, which in turn seems to point to a repetition of history. For example, even in the United States, southerners do not usually read Tocqueville in the same way as Yankees do, and regional differences persist in the United States despite (or because of) the Civil War. For example, Tocqueville could be read as describing two Americas: the one derived from the Puritans, and the other steeped in the aristocratic culture of the Old South that promoted slavery. In his postmodern treatise *America*, Jean Baudrillard writes (1986:88):

> Tocqueville describes the beneficial effects of democracy and the American constitution with considerable enthusiasm . . . he then describes with equal lucidity the extermination of the Indians and the condition of the Negroes . . . as if good and evil had developed separately. . . . What has become of this paradoxical grandeur, the New World's original situation as described by Tocqueville? What has become of this American revolution that consisted in the dynamic resolution of a clearly understood individual interest and a well-tempered collective morality?

Up to the postmodernist era of the 1980s, Tocqueville has been read primarily from a northern, modernist, assimilatory context. Now that secession, rebellion, and civil war are raging in post-Communist lands, one is afforded an opportunity to read Tocqueville in a different way and to extend tocqueville's relevance to a new context.

Specifically, we shall suggest that Tocqueville's depiction of the two Americas—North and South, Puritan and aristocratic, respectively—leads to the awareness that there might exist two opposing cultures in what used to be Yugoslavia. For a long time, convention has made one used to thinking of one America, one Yugoslavia, and even one Soviet Union. The American Civil War suggests that Tocqueville was correct to suggest that American might be regarded more accurately as the sometimes unhappy union of two distinct and opposing cultures. Similarly, one should consider the claim of Tomašić (1941, 1946, 1948a, 1948b, 1951, 1953) that Slavic cultures are dominated by a power-hungry social character that has led to Communism, versus a more peaceable, democratic social type.

The conceptual linkage we wish to make is between the power-hungry Slavic type of social character that reproduced an aristocracy within Communism and Tocqueville's description of the southern aristocrat. Tocqueville wrote ([1845] 1945:410): "The citizen of the Southern states becomes a sort of domestic dictator from infancy; the first notion he acquires in life is that he is born to command, and the first habit which he contracts is that of ruling without resistance. His education tends, then, to give him the character of a haughty and hasty man, irascible, violent, ardent in his desires, impatient of obstacles, but easily discouraged if he cannot succeed upon his first attempt." It is remarkable that Tomašić (1948b:92–105) ascribes similar character traits to the citizens of the Dinaric and Ural alps in Slavic lands: an aristocratic respect for power, authoritarianism, an unstable personality structure that lends itself easily to violence.

Tocqueville writes that "the American of the South is fond of grandeur, luxury, and renown, of gayety, pleasure, and, above all, of idleness" ([1845] 1945:411). Again, Tomašić's Dinaric and Ural social types also display a penchant for what Veblen (1899) called the wasteful habits of the leisure class.

Tocqueville ascribes these differences between North and South to the vastly different habits of the heart of the groups of settlers that came to inhabit the two regions. The North was settled by educated, talented, and family-oriented citizens, whereas the South was settled by "speculators and adventurers greedy of gain," not to mention some convicts (Tocqueville [1845] 1945:32). Thus, "The immigrants of New England brought with them the best elements of order and morality; they landed on the desert coast accompanied by their wives and children" (p. 33). In general, there can be little doubt that Tocqueville ascribes the core of the "good" America to a tiny kernel in New England (p. 32):

> In the English colonies of the North, more generally known as the New England states, the two or three main ideas that now constitute the basis of the social theory of the United States were first combined. The principles of New England spread at first to the neighboring states; they then passed successively to the more distant ones; and at last, if I may so speak, they interpenetrated the whole confederation. They now extend their influence beyond its limits, over the whole American world. *The civilization of New England has been like a beacon lit upon a hill, which, after it has diffused its warmth immediately around it, also tinges the distant horizon with its glow* [emphasis added].

Tocqueville believed that the North was influenced by the intellect, whereas the South accepted the germs of aristocracy (p. 48). The aristocratic element led to slavery and idleness, but it also tended toward heroism and war; the American aristocrats were "the class which headed the insurrection in the South and furnished the best leaders of the American Revolution" (p. 49). He felt that the Puritan, intellectual influence extended "east of the Hudson," whereas "in most of the states situated to the southwest of the Hudson some great English proprietors had settled who had imported with them aristocratic principles" (p. 49).

It is interesting that many of these same traits can still be ascribed to male residents of the southern United States, compared with those in the North. Yet, there exists an important difference between the fate of the democratic experiment on this side of the Atlantic versus that in the Slavic lands. The aristocratic cultural element seems to be stronger in what used to be Communist countries —and Communism itself became a sort of aristocracy, despite the rhetoric of equality. This is not to deny that aristocracy might not have been victorious in the United States. The South might have won,[2] and even though it lost, there exists widespread nostalgia for the values that the South represents. Witness the tremendous popularity of *Gone with the Wind* and its sequel, *Scarlett,* books that have sold more copies than any other except the Bible. (Furthermore, the cinematic version of *Gone with the Wind* has been the most popular film of all time.) The important point is that Slavic beacons of democracy were never as powerful as the beacon from New England that is described by Tocqueville.

Tocqueville reviews many differences in habits of the heart between the North and South to arrive at the following analogy and conclusion ([1845] 1945:412): "If two men are united in society who have the same interests, and, to a certain extent, the same opinions, but different characters, different acquirements, and a different style of civilization, it is most probable that these men will not agree. The same remark is applicable to a society of nations. Slavery, then, does not attack the American Union directly in its interests, but indirectly in its manners." This is a fascinating interpretation of the true causes of the American Civil War as being fundamentally cultural, although the United States is not our primary focus. The more important point, for the purposes of the present discussion, is that Tocqueville's analysis is analogous to Tomašić's analysis of opposing character types in Slavic lands: one should not have expected the Serbs and Croats to agree on how to live in a federated Yugoslavia, given their vastly different habits of the heart. If Tocqueville is right that the American Civil War was preordained because of the radically different cultural traits that he uncovered, then the Yugoslav civil war that began in 1991 was similarly predestined. This is the avenue, at least, that we wish to pursue.

One has a right to question whether Tocqueville's distinction is still applicable in the 1990s, and the most reasonable reply seems to be that it is probably less applicable than it was in the 1840s. Nevertheless, the South has maintained higher rates of homicide, poverty, and general backwardness that cannot be dismissed (Gastil 1971).[3] The America of the 1840s perhaps corresponds more closely to the relatively less-developed Balkans of the 1990s. The Dinaric and Ural social types described by Tomašić (1948b) display a cultural tendency toward insurrection and violence. For example, it is well known in Yugoslavia that Serbs and Montenegrins adhere to a sort of cult of the warrior. They have continually dominated the police and armed forces. They habitually own guns and engage in hunting as part of a machismo set of values. Within Yugoslavia, they are known for being stubborn, irascible, and emotionally unstable. It is interesting that many of these same traits can still be ascribed to male residents of the southern United States, in comparison with males in the North.

We thus arrive at the following tentative hypothesis: reconstruction following the war of 1991 in Yugoslavia will depend upon furthering the democratic cultural bases and overcoming the aristocratic, even barbaric influences of other cultural bases. Specifically, one could argue that Slovenia and Croatia—even if they offer a mixture of these two ideal types—tend toward Western cultural values in that they display anti-Communist patterns, a Catholic and therefore universalist base, a tendency toward pluralism, a recognition of values pertaining to human rights, European political values, and a willingness to adopt a free-market economy. In contrast, Serbia and Montenegro have espoused neo-Communist orientations, an Orthodox cultural base that tends to share power with government, a tendency toward a unitary state, and tendencies to dominate existing power structures. To claim that reconstruction should follow the Western model is not appreciably different from noting that following the American Civil War, reconstruction followed the cultural values of the more democratic North as compared with the then-aristocratic South, a distinction that Alexis de Tocqueville thought was important in explaining the American experiment in democracy.

National Character and Destiny

Modernists in general and contemporary Americans in particular are not fond of the notion of destiny. It runs contrary to the

American cultural habit of believing in freedom (especially in the North). By contrast, European intellectuals from the previous fin de siècle and the Romantic era were predisposed to think and write in terms of destiny. The very notion of habit implies destiny as opposed to self-conscious freedom (a point that is apparently missed completely by Bellah et al. 1985 in their Americanization of this concept from Tocqueville). From Freud to Oswald Spengler, one finds the notion that individual or national character is somehow predetermined at an early stage of its existence. In writing the following, Tocqueville ([1845] 1945:27) is no exception to this rule:

> We must watch the infant in his mother's arms; we must see the first images which the external world casts upon the dark mirror of his mind, the first occurrences that he witnesses; we must hear the first words which awaken the sleeping powers of thought, and stand by his earliest efforts if we would understand the prejudices, the *habits*, and the passions which will rule his life. *The entire man is, so to speak, to be seen in the cradle of the child. The growth of nations presents something analogous to this; they all bear some marks of their origin.* The circumstances that accompanied their birth and contributed to their development affected the whole term of their being [emphasis added].

Tocqueville's assessment is entirely in keeping with the Freudian approach to individual and social character. Like so many of his contemporaries, Freud believed that one's character is "set" in the first five years of one's life and that there is very little that can alter the personality traits that have been established in childhood. Many critics of Freud indeed disagree vehemently on this issue. Instead of assessing Freud's claim, it is more instructive, for the purposes of the present analysis, to link it with Tocqueville's belief that "if we were able to go back to the elements of states and to examine the oldest monuments of their history, I doubt not that we should discover in them the primal cause of the prejudices, the habits, the ruling passions, and, in short, all that constitutes what is called the national character" (p. 28).

Tocqueville felt that the Puritan versus the aristocratic origins of the North versus the South explain the different habits of the heart exhibited in these regions of the United States, the conflict between which led ultimately to the Civil War. Similarly, we need to trace the oldest historical monuments of the various national groups that compose contemporary, post-Communist nations. For example, the Catholic influences on Croatia and Slovenia versus the Orthodox influences on Serbia and the southern Yugoslav republics would have to figure prominently in such an explanation. Along these same lines, the fact that Croatia and Slovenia were ruled by Austro-Hungary while the Turks dominated Serbia and the southern regions of Yugoslavia has to be important as well.

Even in the 1990s, substantial differences and hostilities exist between citizens of the northern and the southern United States, although since Lincoln's assassination, the United States has embarked on an assimilatory, modernist project whose aim is to make the entire nation homogeneous. For example, many of Meštrović's Texas students refer to northerners as "damned Yankees." Small southern towns still commemorate the Civil War and display the rebel flag. Black Americans in particular have objected to some of the historical monuments that commemorate southern heroes, whom they regard as bigots. One can also still find northerners who mock southerners as being less intelligent, less cultured, and more bigoted than themselves—and who make fun of the distinctively slow, southern drawl and accent.

If one can still find remnants of the cultural differences that Tocqueville had uncovered in America over a century ago, how much more likely that one will find vast cultural differences among the various groups that compose what used to be Yugoslavia, the Soviet Union, and other post-Communist nations. It is instructive in this regard to compare and contrast Abraham Lincoln and Mikhail Gorbachev, two of the greatest liberators of the past two centuries. Both of them represented assimilatory, modernist forces of cosmopolitanism, and both opposed aristocratic, barbaric forces that promoted division. Both leaders attempted to reform an existing system of government rather than call for a revolution. Lincoln's program succeeded, despite his being assassinated by a southerner, whereas Gorbachev failed, even though he gave up his power peacefully. The violent, disruptive, and antidemocratic forces over which Lincoln triumphed are very similar to the forces that have been unleashed in post-Communist lands.

Changing the Political System

Tocqueville portrayed American religion of the 1830s as the conservative force that would balance the doctrine of self-interest and keep it from degenerating into immorality. Interestingly, he does not treat the topic of the army or the military with any theoretical importance. But in the Balkans, the army and the church represent the two most conservative and antiliberal forces. Moreover, without a strong tradition of individualism to balance these conservative forces, both could become dangerous to the establishment of democracy. The army has already demonstrated this trend by siding completely with Serbia and Montenegro in the war of 1991. One should not forget that this army was supposed to defend all Yugoslavs against foreign invasions: instead, it attacked the Slovenes and Croats. In reality, and again as argued by Tomašić (1948b), the function of the army was always ideological, to defend the regime that guarantees its privileges, not to defend the borders of Yugoslavia.

The Catholic church in Slovenia and Croatia is well known as being the most conservative in Europe. The only prodemocratic cause for optimism is that under Vatican direction, the Catholic church is not supposed to interfere overtly in government functions. By contrast, the Orthodox churches in Serbia and Montenegro, as well as what used to be the Soviet Union, have a long history of identifying with and supporting nationalist and governmental causes (Petro 1990). Even if the overtly democratic changes that have been exhibited by Slovenia and Croatia sweep through the rest of the Balkans, the church will probably continue to represent an authoritarian, nontolerant ideology that might supplant similar tendencies from the previous, Communist regime.

A silver lining in the cloud is that in losing access to the federal army, the Slovenes and Croats have also lost a major source of authoritarian ideology. If they remain demilitarized, and if the Vatican continues to steer the Catholic church toward separation from the state, these two new countries have a chance of entering the Western orbit of democratic values. There exists also the very real danger that they will be overwhelmed by the large, formerly federal army that came under Serbian control in 1991. As for the rest of Yugoslavia, maintenance of the third largest army in Europe — an army that was built on ideological loyalty to a power-seeking regime — will obviously work against democratization.

In sum, the great task for the Balkans is to move from a monolithic political orientation to a pluralistic one. They must achieve this shift without the cultural recourse to individualism and human rights as social values that have been established in and derived from Western Enlightenment. Their task is to derive the ideals of liberal democracy from cultural values that tend to stress collective rights, not individual rights, as enshrined in religion, the nation, and even the military. They must learn to develop a politics that appreciates compromise and that does not tend automatically toward war. This will be an enormously difficult task.

The Role of Civil Religion

Drawing on Tocqueville and Durkheim, Robert N. Bellah (1967) popularized the concept of American civil religion as an alloy of traditional religion and ordinary political institutions that cannot be reduced to either phenomenon alone. An important consequence of this concept is that it enables one to appreciate the religious respect with which a nation celebrates its political ideals, heroes, and values, An excellent illustration of this role of religion is afforded by the collective effervescence of the Americans during and following the Gulf War of 1991.

Whereas American patriotism is referred to as American civil religion, there is a tendency for American and Western European writers to refer to Eastern European nationalism as mere tribalism.[4] Very little is known of the civil religions of the various nations that make up the Balkans. It seem logical, following Tocqueville, Durkheim, and Bellah, that all nations should have their own civil religions. Moreover, the civil religions will have negative as well as positive functions. For example, Bellah (1967) points to the extermination of the Indians and to the Vietnam War as unfortunate aspects of American civil religion, but he concludes that overall, its function in American society has been integrative. One would expect something similar in Balkan cultures. The important point is that all of the abstract systems that concern Western intellectuals— the Enlightenment, liberal democracy, Communism—might be construed as civil religions, as intellectual as well as emotional components of culture that are rooted in a particular people's habits of the heart.

In the present regard, it is important to note that Communism was a civil religion that displaced fascism. Like American civil religion, Communism had its heroes, holidays, monuments, and other cultural focal points of celebration and sacrosanct veneration. Thus, the collapse of Communism in some (though not all) regions in the Balkans represents more than the collapse of an economic system (as suggested by Brzezinski 1989) or even a modernist system (as suggested by Bauman 1992:222). It represents also the collapse of a civil religion. As such, its collapse created an identity crisis and created a vacuum of faith. The liberated Balkan people needed and went searching for a new system of faith in populism, nationalism, and other old-fashioned value systems.

When Fukuyama (1992) and others advocate the end of history and the victory of liberal democratic ideals, they assume that the entire world shares the same civil religion of the Enlightenment.

The Balkans, in fact, never experienced periods like the Enlightenment, the Reformation, or even the Renaissance, so that Fukuyama's assumption is unwarranted. Even if they had, their local cultures would have put a local color and interpretation on these grand abstractions (in the same way that France and the United States differ, even if they do share liberal democratic ideals).

It is difficult for Americans to imagine what the collapse of their civil religion would be like, for they have enjoyed it in a relatively uninterrupted fashion for well over two hundred years (with the possible exception of the Civil War). But with regard to the Balkans, the question must be asked: What will be the sociopsychological impact of the collapse of the Communist civil religion, and what local civil religions will replace it? It is evident already that contrary to the expectations of many on this side of the Atlantic, the post-Communist lands are not importing American or Western European civil religions. In line with Tocqueville, they are developing their own. Thus, post-Communist Croatia is developing a civil religion that portrays its past as one of always seeking freedom from oppressive foreigners. It draws on Medjugorje and the Catholic cult of Mary, the independence of the city-state of Dubrovnik, and even its affiliation with the Austro-Hungarian Empire as various elements, among others, that make up this civil religion. Street names have been changed from those that honored Communist heroes to new names that honor Croatian leaders, scientists, and literary figures. Old Croatian vocabulary is being revived, and in general a frantic search for a distinctly Croatian identity is under way.

In contrast, Serbia has aligned itself (1) with a civil religion that sees itself as the protector of the South Slavs, (2) with the Battle of Kosovo, in which the Slavs lost to the Turks in 1389,[5] and (3) with values associated with heroism and valor in war. Non-Serbian heroes are being expunged. For example, Tito was born in Croatia; for this reason, he has been eliminated almost completely from the Serbian vocabulary. There was even talk of removing his body from the cemetery in Belgrade. Furthermore, the fact that centuries ago there existed Orthodox monasteries in what is now Kosovo was used as justification for the Serbian annexation of Kosovo and for documented human rights abuses against the Muslim minority that lives there (Helsinki Watch Committee 1990).

The important point is that there never existed a true Yugoslav identity or civil religion. Yugoslavia is a creation of various pacts and treaties that were important to Western and Soviet victors, from Versailles to Yalta. The fact that the West in general and the United States in particular clung to the idea of Yugoslavia long after war broke out in 1991 bespeaks the ideological tilt of the West and its inability to appreciate the cultures that make up the Balkans.

The problem for the Balkans in the 1990s will be the following: how to integrate the various Balkan civil religions into a European and international framework of political, economic, and other cultural ties; how to build a new, modern society that will not repeat the errors of the old, modern, highly bureaucratized and inhumane society; and how to build a civil society that will not require a strong state. For nongovernment institutions to thrive, a strong yet peaceable civil religion must thrive first.

The Economic Crisis

The general conclusion reached in the West has been that liberal democracy and the market economy form an inseparable unit that can be exported to other lands (Novak 1982; Muravchick 1991). In terms of the cultural framework being used here, this assumption is questionable. First, there exist several democracies in the world that are not practicing true free-market economies, especially Japan and Germany (Stark 1992). Second, these ideological positions overlook the important link uncovered by Max Weber (1904) between Protestant culture and capitalism. Third, they overlook the importance of a stable civil religion that enables the long-term development of both capitalism and democracy. The post-Communist lands today are in crisis, are predominantly non-Protestant, and are starting from a cultural base that is distinct from those that gave rise to liberal democracy and the market economy.

In the Balkans, there does not exist a middle class as it is known in the West. The population is still divided between urbanites and a predominantly peasant population. Balkan intellectuals are the seeds of a new middle class that will take many years to develop. There exists a high concentration of capital in the hands of a limited segment of the population. For example, in Croatia, twenty firms own 80 percent of the resources. Privatization will not ameliorate this tendency but will tend to reward those who are already wealthy, most of whom are former Communists. The ordinary person in the Balkans is unable to purchase the goods of reprivatization and denationalization.

Thus far, all recipes have come from free-market advocates in the West, working in the classical economic paradigms. They advocate the removal of price controls and subsidies, a completely open economy, foreign investments, the closing of inefficient plants, the removal of redundant or inefficient employees, and, overall, the establishment of a supply-side market economy. Such strategies in East Germany, Poland, the former Czechoslovakia, and Russia have so far caused tremendous hardships on the unsuspecting population, including high unemployment, increasing crime rates, mass migration in search of jobs, and family instability. Some of the Western vices that the Communists had warned against are making inroads into Eastern and Central Europe, among them, stress, drugs, alcoholism, prostitution, and crime.

In Durkheimian terms, a condition of anomie is being introduced unwittingly into post-Communist lands. Durkheim (1897) taught that anomie is promoted by a combination of weakened social regulatory mechanisms coupled with heightened desires for gain and other passions. This is exactly what has occurred throughout Eastern Europe and the Balkans. The rapid change in governments, civil religions, and other regulatory mechanisms has caused disorientation, *déclassement*, even *dérèglement* at the same time that consumer appetites for Western goods has increased dramatically. Unless the social and cultural balance is restored, there exists every danger that the Durkheimian consequences will follow in the Balkans as well: even more crime, suicide, and other undesirable behaviors.

In sum, we contend that post-Communism is a unique situation in the world in that it involves pre-Communist cultural traditions that are being exposed to Western, postmodernist, and consumer-oriented forces. We predict that a new type of social structure will emerge eventually, but not until the Balkans experience some of the social ills associated with postmodern culture that the ideologues tend not to mention. These social ills include narcissism, extreme cultural relativism, a breakdown of social norms and traditions, and other anomic tendencies (see Bellah et al. 1985; Bloom 1987; Lasch 1991; Meštrović 1991).

Implications

We have deliberately compared Tocqueville with Tomašić in order to lay the groundwork for what follows, and in order to capture the gist of the post-Communist world scene. Post-Communism is upsetting the modernist dreams of the end of history, nationalism, religion, tradition, and differences among peoples of the world. Post-Communist nations began to turn to their habits of the heart and to emphasize their differences almost as soon as they were freed from the modernist yoke of Communism. In order to emphasize that not all habits of the heart are benign or destructive, we invoked Tocqueville to make the point that they are both good and bad. This aspect of Tocqueville has been obfuscated in modernist readings of him, and we had to highlight it in order to proceed with the present discussion.

One scenario for the future of post-Communist lands seems to dominate Western media as well as intellectual treatises, namely, that market economy, democracy, and pluralism will prevail. This scenario is commensurate with Fukuyama's thesis that with the alleged fall of Communism, the West has witnessed the end of history. We disagree with this thesis on the straightforward grounds that Balkanization, nationalism, and territorial imperialism—humanity's historical vices—have reappeared in post-Communist lands in the past two years. But because facts do not and cannot speak for themselves, a cultural explanation was sought as the basis for explaining the West's optimistic hopes as well as the failure so far of the post-Communist lands to live up to those hopes.

Fukuyama's thesis assumes one universal history that can be studied in a scientific manner, a position in keeping with the faith in the Enlightenment that has prevailed in the West. However, for the sake of objectivity, by which we mean addressing opposing theories and points of view, we decided to invoke postmodern and sociocultural points of view. For the postmodernists, the Enlightenment is oppressive, not liberating. There exist *many* histories in the world, and each is rooted to a people's culture. We touched on cultural theorists from Tocqueville to Bellah to highlight the view that a culture is rooted in a people's habits of the heart and does not exist a priori, as a pure abstraction.[6]

Using these many points of view, we exposed a number of other lacunae in the prevalent, Western attitude toward the fall of Communism and its aftermath. First, the Western optimism and faith in liberal democracy, the end of history, and the market are phenomena peculiar to the modernist West and are not universal hard facts. Second, we suggested that the West's attitude betrays a sort of imperialism on ideological and other nonmilitary grounds. In other words, up to now, the West has assumed the assimilatory forces of modernization would work on its behalf. Third, and closely related, we noted that Western analysts seem uninterested in attaining a *cultural* understanding of the habits of the heart of the people who were ruled by Communism, who are now assumed to be willing recipients of the fruits of modern, Western *civilization*. Finally, and relying on contemporary cultural analysts of American culture (among them Bellah, Lasch, and Riesman), we noted problems with contemporary liberal democracy in the United States, including narcissism, excessive consumerism, paralyzing cultural relativism, cynicism, and continued problems with race relations, among others. Again, we leave for another discussion the question whether these problems are cultural or universal.

Nevertheless, once the analyst is able to step outside the much-vaunted Western scenario, other possible scenarios for the future of post-Communist lands emerge. These include Balkanization, conflict, isolation, separation, the emergence of new nations, chaos, and perhaps even the rise of new forms of totalitarianism. Some of these negative and undesirable scenarios are supported by an examination of the history of the post-Communist lands, which is replete with these phenomena. Others are supported by a straightforward comparison with the history of the West, which hardly constitutes an instance of straight-line progress. If Tocqueville and Baudrillard are correct that there exists a "good" as well as a "bad" America, there is no reason to suppose that something similar might not apply to the cultures that survived Communism. In addition, it must be noted that the newly liberated Slavic cultures tend to lack the Reformation as well as the Enlightenment tradition, widely regarded as essential to the progress of democracy as well as capitalism in the West. This is not to conclude that Slavic cultures lack a peaceable cultural base that might serve to promote democracy and the free market, only that (1) these might not be exactly the same as our versions of the same phenomena, and (2) we know next to nothing of the habits of the heart of the Slavic people. Western sociologists and other analysts of culture are guilty of a long-standing preoccupation with themselves and of ignoring the Balkans, Russia, and other post-Communist lands.

In addition, the lack of understanding and communication between the West and the newly liberated nations may itself contribute to the negative scenarios. When post-Communist nations fail to live up to Western expectations, the result is not always one that is in keeping with the high image that the West has of itself as rational. Consider, for example, former U.S. Ambassador to Yugoslavia

(1981–85) David Anderson's cruel dismissal of all the Yugoslavs when they turned to war instead of looking out for their rational self-interest, as conceived by the West: "The problem, I fear, is the Yugoslavs themselves. They are a perverse group of folks, near tribal in their behavior, suspicious of each other (with usually sound reasons), friendly on the outside but very cynical within, ever ready for a war or a battle, proud of their warrior history, and completely incapable of coming to grips with the modern world. . . . So, I would say, a plague on both houses [the Croats and the Serbs]."[7]

The West continued to mourn the dissolution of Communist Yugoslavia well into 1992, even though only Serbia and Montenegro apparently wish to preserve it. The United States in particular refused to go along with the European Community and forty-three other nations who recognized the independence of Slovenia and Croatia on January 16, 1992. It seems that the return of history in the Balkans was too sharp a departure from Fukuyama's predictions to be acceptable to the United States. The Slovenes and the Croatians, in turn, felt betrayed by the United States and began to express public suspicions about the discrepancy between America's *actions* to preserve the status quo or further its self-interest,[8] cited earlier by Toynbee (1962:92), versus its *rhetoric* of supporting freedom and democracy.

In sum, our cultural approach calls for the establishment of genuine dialogue among the various histories and cultures that are involved, in the East and West, in the transition from Communism to liberal democracy. The West should not assume that one brand of democracy, its own, fits all. It should seek, instead, to understand the habits of the heart of the newly freed nations. The East needs to understand the modern, Western focus on self-interest and its consequences. Bellah and Tocqueville should be read in Belgrade and Moscow, but Tomašić and Spengler should be read in Washington, D.C. Empathetic understanding is needed by all, not simplistic slogans about winning the Cold War on one side and paranoid nationalism that leads to violence on the other.

In must be emphasized that we are not dismissing the possibility of democracy and the free market in post-Communist lands. Our essential point, however, is that democracy and the free market are not free-floating, ahistorical abstractions but are rooted in culture. Thus, Bellah et al. (1985) may be right that America needs to reexamine the habits of the heart that made it a revolutionary example for the world. This return by America into its own history entails an honest appraisal of its good as well as its bad cultural traits. Similarly, there can be no doubt that post-Communist cultures contain their own unique blends of good versus bad habits of the heart. Our conclusion is that the good, peaceable, prodemocratic habits that lead to liberty should be nurtured, while the negative ones should be examined and restrained. The moral restraint must occur spontaneously, by the people themselves, not by social engineers working for governments, universities, and corporations. Otherwise, the evils of the Bolsheviks, who were masters at social engineering, might be imposed again upon an unsuspecting, newly freed people.

3. The Aristocratic Temperament in the Balkans

Tomašić argues that there exist some Eastern European and other Slavic types of social character that are not conducive to the Western notions of democracy or free-market economy. Moreover, this power-seeking, Slavic type of personality structure may explain why before, during, and, in some cases, following Communism, age-old patterns of authoritarianism, power-seeking, and autocratic rule have persisted. Writing in 1948, Tomašić claimed that "the clash between Soviet totalitarian socialism and Western liberalism is nothing but a new form of an old struggle that has ravaged Eastern Europe for 2,000 years" (1948b:9). This is a provocative thesis.

Tomašić claims that his analysis applies especially to the "mountain people" who live in Yugoslavia, Romania, Bulgaria, Greece, Albania, Poland, and portions of old Russia. The shepherds and other herdsmen who inhabited the Dinaric Alps and the Ural Mountains are especially prone to undemocratic tendencies, according to Tomašić. With regard to the Yugoslavs, Tomašić traces undemocratic forces among the Dinaric inhabitants of both Croatia and Serbia but believes that the Serbs—before, during, and following Communism in Yugoslavia—exhibited more of these barbaric character traits than the Croats did: "But since the Serbian ruling classes followed Ural-Altaic and Byzantine traditions of limitless power, they insisted on a centralistic organization of the State and rigid concentration of all power in their own hands" (1948b:132).

More specifically, Tomašić followed Cvijic (1931), an anthropologist and geographer, and Dvorniković (1931), a psychologist, in delineating three distinct types of social character operating in Yugo-slavia as well as the Soviet Union: the power-hungry, aggressive Rodopian-Dinaric or Ural herdsman; the peaceable, rural-plains farmer; and the urban-industrial cosmopolitan type. The last two possess a social character that is more conducive to Western out-looks. While Tomašić concentrates on the aggressive social type, he emphasizes that the other, more peaceable and cosmopolitan types —the farmers and the urban dwellers—offset the brutality of the Dinaric types and other herdsmen. The only problem is that the peaceable types are not as interested in politics as the power-seeking types, which leads to the instability and political turmoil that is characteristic of the Balkans. He also links the power-hungry type of social character to the result of centuries of Turkish domination and other Oriental influences in the Balkans.

More contemporary, general support for Tomašić's claims can be found in works by Augustin (1974), Klaić (1978), Lucev (1974), and St. Erlich (1973, 1974), among others, who have found that the remote and mountainous regions of Yugoslavia indeed might be characterized as being less conducive to democracy than the plains and the urban centers.[1] The central importance of Tomašić's argu-ment is that it helps to explain the details surrounding the Yugoslav War of 1991—between Bosnia-Hercegovina, Croatia, and Slovenia seeking independence versus Serbia and Montenegro seeking to pre-serve the old power structure—as well as the events that led up to it. In particular, Tomašić's theory helps to explain the Serbian de-sire to gain territory at Croatia's expense, its human rights abuses in Kosovo, its clinging to Communism, although most of Eastern Europe voted for Democratic forms of government, and the fact that the government bureaucracy of what used to be Communist Yugo-slavia was dominated by Serbs.[2]

The Reception of Tomašić's Theory

In addition to the two books we have already cited, Tomašić published on various aspects of his theory in widely respected sociological journals, among them the *American Sociological Review* and the *American Journal of Sociology*. Overall, the reviews of his 1948 book are much more favorable than those of the 1953 book. It must be kept in mind that Tomašić wrote during the era that witnessed the beginnings of the Cold War, so that his *cultural* explanation was drowned out by the *ideological* explanations that were becoming increasingly popular. Moreover, the anthropological approach that Tomašić used, which is very close to the theories of Ruth Benedict, was itself in decline following World War II, as noted by David Riesman (1964) and others.

Writing in response to Tomašić's *Personality and Culture in Eastern European Politics*, Stephen W. Mamchur wrote in the *American Sociological Review* (1948:326):

> As an essentially psychiatric explanation of politics in this area [the Balkans] rather than one in terms of balance of power or such symptom-phenomena as the megalomania of a particular potentate, this study is an outstanding and distinctive contribution to social science theory as well as to an understanding of this area. While it contains a few minor negative aspects, the study is, on the whole, an invaluable combination of the psychiatric and cultural approaches in the analysis of literate societies relatively little known in the West.

Mamchur added that Tomašić's study should prove valuable "to statesmen who attempt to establish peace and freedom in the powder-keg of Europe." It seems that this statement still applies to the Balkans.

Reviewing the same book, John J. Honigman wrote in *Social Forces* that the sort of unstable, Dinaric culture described by Tomašić "is the kind of society which Ruth Benedict has described in lectures as promoting humiliation and frustration so that interpersonal hostility must follow as a consequence" (1949:349). He criticizes Tomašić for overgeneralizing "from his Yugoslav sample to other Balkan countries as well as to Poland." This is certainly a valid criticism, one we have encountered earlier with regard to Tocqueville's generalizations. However, in defense of Tomašić, one could counter that in fact the countries that concerned Tomašić—Yugoslavia,

Bulgaria, Albania, Romania, Hungary, the former Czechoslovakia, and Poland—did in fact remain Communist and display the power-seeking traits that he described well up to 1989. If even one or several of these countries had broken free from Communism earlier, one might be more prone to criticize Tomašić. In sum, his generalization proved to be remarkably accurate.

Another review of this book is found in the *American Journal of Sociology*, authored by Otakar Machotka (1949:105), whose summary is worth citing if only to compare it with ours:

> The restless, fighting, rough, and highly ambitious political behavior of certain eastern Europeans originates in the Dinaric element of the population. Though the Dinarics are not the major component of the population, their strong political interest and ambition as well as their relatively poor economic resources push them, more than other elements of the population, into the political life. Since the strongest element, the peasants, are peaceful and not interested in public affairs, the Dinarics easily dominate the local political life.

It is worth noting that this characterization applies to the Yugoslav case up the present. For example, the Montenegrins, who are the poorest and most backward people in what used to be Yugoslavia, had a national reputation for dominating the police and military forces numerically and in terms of rank well out of proportion to their population. Machotka evaluates Tomašić as follows: "It is a great merit of the book that it explains political happenings by a certain basic, generally widespread type of personality. This approach, so needed in the analysis of political events, is far from being generally accepted and understood. Economic causes and political ideologies are mostly the leading principles of explanation, the social-psychological causes being very often completely forgotten."

Turning next to the review of Tomašić's *Impact of Russian Culture on Soviet Communism* (1953), N. S. Timasheff wrote in the *American Sociological Review* (1953:725): "Commonly, these problems are approached from the angle of view of the impact of the dynamic force of Communism on the relatively stable Russian culture. Mr. Tomašić has chosen to make a study in reverse and to find out what has been the impact of Russian culture on Communism." Timasheff has located what is distinctive, and still relevant, in Tomašić's approach. For if we break "Communism" and "Bolshevism" into their constituent parts, such as totalitarianism, dictatorship, lack of freedom, primitivism, and so on, it now seems obvious —with the wisdom of hindsight—that most of these elements can be found in the political and social procedures that *preceded* Communism. Without Tomašić's cultural approach, one is forced to make the logically absurd argument that Communism is self-begotten, that it developed suddenly of its own accord. Timasheff summarizes Tomašić as claiming that the power-hungry and democratic aspects of Russian culture have never been merged successfully; "hence something akin to split personality is considered to have been the dominant trait of the Russian culture" (p. 726).

In the rest of his review, Timasheff criticizes Tomašić for not supplying the evidence of a matriarchal, peaceable cultural force from Slavic prehistory. From the perspective of the present discussion, the most interesting point about this criticism is that it applies to Veblen, Bachofen, Jung, Erich Fromm, and a number of others who posit a mythical, matriarchal past. It is not certain that this controversy will be resolved finally, but it is not important to Tomašić's argument. The important point is that Tomašić characterizes Slavic culture in this schizophrenic way.

Timasheff raises another objection in this regard, namely, that Tomašić classifies traits as belonging either "to the gentle culture of the old Slavs or to the ferocious culture of the Turko-Mongol," and that he does so "in an impressionistic manner." Actually, what appears to be impressionism is a theoretical perspective shared by Veblen and a number of other theorists—namely, that the human animal is a *homo duplex*, peaceable as well as barbaric. We shall have more to say on this later. At this point in the discussion, it is important only to point out that the significance of Tomašić's theory lies in its effort to offer a cultural explanation of events that are typically understood in strictly ideological, economic, or otherwise reductionistic ways.

Other Controversies

As stated from the outset, we realize that interpreting the Yugoslav War that began in 1991, as well as other post-Communist developments, through theories that involve the notion of social character in general and Tomašić in particular are bound to be controversial. But partial support for Tomašić's contentious claims can be found in U.S. Senate Resolution 176, sponsored by Senator Dole and passed on September 11, 1991. This resolution specifically "condemns the policies of violent aggression perpetrated by Serbian President Slobodan Milošević, the Yugoslav Army and Serbian extremist guerillas in Croatia," and it "condemns the continuing and increasing repression against the Albanian population in the Province of Kosovo" that had been perpetrated by the Serbs for over three years. In sum, the U.S. Senate's own investigative efforts into the conflict between Croatia and Serbia that began in 1991 led it to side with relatively more democratic Croatia and against hard-line, Communist Serbia. Senators Robert Dole, Albert Gore, and Alphonse D'Amato, as well as Congressman Christopher Smith, among other United States politicians who became involved in trying to broker peace in Yugoslavia in 1991, all noticed that the Serbian hard-liners seemed to talk peace at the same time that they waged a particularly brutal war. Thus, we should not dismiss Tomašić's claims concerning Serbia out of hand simply because they tend to be critical and take a stand. The Western communications media noted repeatedly that Serbia represented Communist, federalist, and aggressive tendencies toward all its neighbors except the Montenegrins in the late 1980s and early 1990s. The new dimension we are bringing to this discussion is the notion that Serbia's expansionist tendencies may reflect the dominance of the aggressive, power-hungry social character uncovered by Tomašić at the expense of the peaceable social character that also exists in Serbia.

Another contentious aspect of Tomašić's claim is the association of aggressive, power-hungry tendencies with peoples who inhabit mountainous regions or who make a livelihood as herdsmen. While this connection has not been proven conclusively and perhaps cannot be proven according to positivistic standards (because all such findings are contingent and subject to further revision), the more important point is that there exists suggestive evidence to support Tomašić's claims. A recent study by Thomas Sowell (1991) emphasizes the role of geography and location in the ways that cultures can borrow from each other or are insulated, pointing out that peoples of the world who live in mountainous regions tend to be more insulated and isolated. This may explain the general backwardness and inability to borrow innovations that is found among many mountain peoples, especially, for the purposes of the present discussion, among the isolated eastern and southern stretches of what used to be the Soviet Union, and the extremely isolated Dinaric regions of Yugoslavia. Certainly it is worth noting that following the collapse of Communism in the late 1980s, fighting broke out in the Balkans, Georgia, Azerbaijan, and other remote regions of the Urals.

We do not wish to hypothesize that remote mountainous regions tend to produce power-seeking personalities. That would be a positivistic effort at grand theorizing that is beside the point and is certainly not our aim. The more important point is that the Dinaric and Ural alps have been and continue to be hot spots in the world and that these facts are at least highlighted by Tomašić's theory.

Still another objection might be that Tomašić's theories might have been applicable a century ago but that surely in the 1990s, modern roads and communication in the Balkans have eliminated the sort of isolation described above. Two factors must be weighed in this regard. First, the Dinaric regions being discussed are still much more isolated and have less access to paved roads and modern communication than do the rest of the Balkans. Second, even if the youngest generation and every succeeding generation becomes more democratic and less ethnocentric by virtue of being exposed to more points of view, the politicians, soldiers, and other authority figures currently in power in the Balkans were raised under the older, more backward conditions and relative isolation. Thus, even if modernization works against the trends uncovered by Tomašić and others, it would be a mistake to assume too much modernization by the Balkans: this region remains the most backward, isolated, and poverty stricken in Europe.

Tomašić (1948b) makes much of the fact that the Dinaric types were associated along patrimonial and patriarchal family units called the *zadruga*, which is essentially an extended family in which the sons never leave. The division of the zadrugas led to many interfamily conflicts over property but came to be associated in general with a violent predisposition. Even the most important founding father of sociology, Emile Durkheim, observed this tendency a century ago in book reviews he wrote on the zadruga (in Nandan 1980:199–316 passim). More recently, Paige (1974) found that patrilocal societies scored high on violence compared with matrilocal and neolocal patterns of residence.

Along these lines, Lott and Hart (1977) point to a psychological connection between the aggression that must be displayed toward animals by mountain-dwelling herdsmen and the aggression they show toward each other. Whiting and Whiting (1975) draw similar connections between the lack of intimacy between husband and wife, who typically do not share the same bed in such cultures, and the general sense of aloofness necessary to survive as a herdsman. Connections between mountain-dwelling herdsmen and warlike tendencies abound in the sociological literature (e.g., see Gallais 1972 and Karan 1977).

Even within the contemporary United States, many studies suggest that the Appalachian and Rocky Mountain regions are distinctly more violent, crime ridden, and barbaric relative to the other regions, especially when compared with the peaceable Midwest, which boasts the lowest homicide rates in the country (see Stark 1991). But in general, we leave open the specific, anthropological, psychological, and sociological reasons why the herdsmen who populate the mountainous regions of Eastern Europe, the Balkans, and the USSR—specifically the Dinaric and Ural mountains—might be more likely than other groups to develop an antidemocratic culture. We have shown that some contemporary studies suggest that there does exist some sort of affinity between antidemocratic cultural traits and living in remote mountainous regions, even though the explanations for this connection are not conclusive. For the purposes of the present discussion, which involve making sense of post-Communist developments in Yugoslavia, it is not necessary to understand these causal mechanisms in a positivistic sense (nor to assume that a final understanding shall ever emerge). Rather, the important point is that Tomašić's claims should not be dismissed out of hand because they rely on generalizations about peoples and on the controversial notion of social character.

In addition to the empirical support for Tomašić that we have cited above, one should note theoretical support as well. Thus, one should note that Veblen (1899, 1917) made much of the connection between predatory "habits of the fight" and living the life of a mountainous herdsman, whether one herded sheep or cattle. For example, he discussed specifically the Aryan herdsmen who instigated the caste system in India and whose barbaric tendencies were later revived by the Nazis. Even if this connection cannot be falsified according to positivistic standards, it is interesting that even in the West's cultural collective representations, the images of the cowboy reverberate with images of the barbarian. One thinks of the question posed in the musical film *Oklahoma*, "Can the farmer and the cowboy be friends?" That is the question, still unresolved, which Veblen, Tomašić, and other students of culture ask us to address.

Another point of remarkable theoretical convergence between Veblen and Tomašić is that both held a view of Western, modern culture as being simultaneously barbaric and peaceable. For example, with regard to Veblen, David Riesman (1964:391) notes that

Veblen made the daring claim that "modern society was in its essential tone, only a latter-day barbarism." This means that the Balkans are not unique relative to the purportedly more civilized West. Rather, the Balkans exhibit more extremely the opposition between barbaric and peaceable traits that is found all over the world.

Contemporary Relevance of Tomašić's Observations

The Western news media's coverage of various aspects of the war in former Yugoslavia that began in 1991 supports many of Tomašić's depictions of Dinaric and particularly Serbian social character. For example, in the New York Times, one reads that "the Serbs have earned a reputation for ferocity" (May 21, 1992:A14). In particular, John F. Burns writes that "the level of unreason seems greatest among the 'divljaci,' the wild men from the remote mountain areas of Bosnia who predominate among the militia groups" (New York Times, May 24, 1992:E4). In another article, Burns argues that the "mountain men" who committed most of the atrocities in the contemporary war see themselves as survivors of Chetnik bands who had committed similar atrocities during World War II (May 31, 1992:A1).

Tomašić's claim that the Dinaric types exhibit heightened paranoia is supported by the observation that in the Serbian media, "Western nations are portrayed as devils out to persecute the poor misunderstood Serbs" (New York Times, June 5, 1992:A8). The lack of restraint that concerned Tomašić is found in the merciless Serbian attacks on civilian populations: "The whole idea of the attack is to humiliate, to punish and to subjugate the population" (June 9, 1992:A1). Indeed, "what characterizes this conflict is the willingness of armies to attack civilians as the main form of warfare" (June 18, 1992:A1). Michael T. Kaufman adds: "Why the Serbs are using so much firepower to destroy their targets is something that baffles visitors to places like Mostar or . . . most particularly, to Vukovar" (p. A4).

Systematic, repeated deceit has played a major role in the Yugoslav war. Burns writes in the *New York Times:* "'The whole world must know by now that the [Serbian] Chetniks are liars,' said the Commander of Gorazde's volunteer army. . . . 'They have constantly lied in the past, and anybody who believes that they are going to stop their killing now should know that they are still lying' he added." (June 20, 1992:A1)[3]

As another illustration of Tomašić's claim, Slaven Letica (1990) has found that most of the recently democratically elected officials in Croatia were born and raised in the Dinaric Alps region of Yugoslavia. The fact that they were elected democratically and did not seize power by force seems to speak against Tomašić. Letica's point, though, is that politicians are concerned with power in general, whether they seize it democratically or not, and it is interesting that even in post-Communist, democratic Croatia, the politicians are more likely to be descended from herdsmen and shepherds than from farmers who make a living in non-Dinaric regions.

Tomašić elaborates that in the ideal-type Slavic family from the Dinaric Alps, the father is authoritarian and power hungry yet beset by ambivalence; women are subservient yet idolized; and children learn either to identify with the father or to rebel against him as well as all subsequent authority at the same time that they develop a passive character orientation. Often, hate rather than love predominates in husband-wife and parent-child relations. It is intriguing that many of Tomašić's descriptions overlap with those in Erich Fromm's portrait of Mexican peasant social character traits (see Fromm and Maccoby 1970) as well as Veblen's (1899) analyses of the predatory "habits of the fight" that have survived into modernity.

According to Tomašić, this Dinaric type of family organization leads to specific, predictable personality traits, some of which may seem desirable from Western perspectives, and others not, namely, a fixation on guilt; a zero-sum mentality[4] in which small failures are interpreted as catastrophes and ordinary successes as grand events; cynicism, mistrust, and deep-seated suspiciousness of the motives of others; a tendency to rebel at authority instead of working with it; the belief that the most important thing in life is power, coupled with a seemingly contradictory sense of compassion for the powerless; a spiritual, fatalistic, and even existential outlook; and the tendency toward extreme self-sacrifice to achieve one's goals.

One of Tomašić's most disturbing observations is that "the Dinarics can hate with a consuming passion and a violence that reaches a white heat" (1948b:35). One thinks of the hatred that has been expressed between some Croats and Serbs in the war that began in 1991 as a contemporary illustration of Tomašić's claim. Americans in particular and Western Europeans in general seem unable to comprehend the intensity of hatred between these two ethnic groups. This is not to claim that hatred and barbarism are unknown in modern nations, but that in the modern West, these phenomena are muted, controlled, and perhaps sublimated (Elias 1982). By contrast, the Yugoslav civil war exhibited barbaric acts of cruelty—massacres and the mutilation of the living as well as corpses—that were so savage and gross that they beg for an explanation. Our explanation is that when one examines the history of the Balkans, such savagery appears to be fairly typical.

As another illustration of the continued relevance of at least some of Tomašić's assertions, consider that the most common complaint made by contemporary American businesses trying to establish themselves in post-Communist Eastern Europe is that Eastern Europeans do not possess a true work ethic and that they do not understand the American idea that economic success for some must necessarily entail failure for others (see Clemens 1989; Drucker 1990; Kempe 1990). In the United States, if one fails at an endeavor, one tries again and again, and eventually, it is believed, one will succeed at something, although not necessarily at the original goal. In Dinaric culture, failure is catastrophe, something like the Oriental losing face. It evokes feelings of guilt, fatalism, and worthlessness, as well as despair. It is worth exploring how such an attitude is transmitted in families and schools, and the role it plays in the workplace. How can the Slavic lands incorporate a "success ethic"?

For example, data suggest that during the Communist phase, the average Yugoslav worked three hours out of a typical eight-hour work day. The rest of the time was spent taking coffee breaks and "wasting time" (from Max Weber's perspective). To the cynical rejoinder that Westerners waste time as well, one needs to point out that Westerners commonly work more than eight hours per day (especially if they are professionals) and that most who are able to work in the family are employed in some fashion. By contrast, visitors to Eastern Europe know that if they visit a restaurant or typical shop, they are more likely not to be served or helped than to encounter the friendly, American, "May I help you?" Yugoslavs, in particular, interpret all failure as catastrophe, and success in general as a zero-sum event. Eastern Europeans in general cannot comprehend why capitalism must entail layoffs, job insecurity, and business failures, because all these things are interpreted as being catastrophic in Dinaric culture.[5]

David Riesman has remarked that what amazed him when he was in the Soviet Union as a youngster in the summer of 1931 was that anything worked at all, especially outside of Moscow and Leningrad.[6] One can still be surprised that things continue to work at all in the former Soviet Union, many portions of Eastern Europe, and especially the Balkans. Again, one could respond with the counter that even in the United States, some people work fearfully hard and show off the long hours they put into their jobs, while others "soldier" on the job and sabotage it, like students who do not want to see the curve raised. But even if one grants that productivity in the United States could be higher and better compared with present standards, any visitor to the formerly Communist nations knows that one cannot really compare the United States with them. In the former USSR and Eastern Europe, it often seems to be a major achievement to place a telephone call, find an apartment, secure medical help, even purchase a postage stamp, among other things that are still routine in the West. Our point is that these obstacles to efficiency might not stem from a lack of resources, incentive, or other modernist factors, but from the dominance of a particular type of social character.

In sum, Tomašić argues that a relatively consistent but destructive type of social character has persisted in the Balkan and Slavic lands since the days of Genghis Khan. To repeat, he concentrates on the power-hungry type of social character that has dominated Slavic politics for many centuries, not on the "good" types of social character. It is important to note that other groups in Slavic lands tend to be more democratic and indeed offset the nondemocratic tendencies of the barbaric descendants of Genghis Khan. But overall, he claims that the Ural horsemen have left a legacy that makes it difficult for democracy or free-market economies to take root, while it is conducive to repeated tyrannical forms of government: "The states dominated by warriors and policemen give full rein to the traditional ideals of Dinaric culture, and their condition presages an era of acute conflict" (1948b:14). Has Eastern Europe in general and the Balkans in particular entered this era of acute conflict? And do they foreshadow an even bloodier conflict that might result in the former USSR as its various nationalities attempt to forge a new commonwealth? These are the sorts of questions to which Tomašić's analysis points, which we think will become increasingly important as the century draws to a close.

Disorganization and Oedipal Conflicts

According to Tomašić, Dinaric family discipline constantly alternates between the extremes of harshness and indulgence, which favors the development of a malevolent, deceitful, and disorderly view of the universe and an emotionally unbalanced, violent, rebellious, and power-seeking personality. These personality traits, in turn, lead to tense interpersonal and cultural relationships and to extreme political instability. For example, in extremely backward, mountainous regions of Montenegro—a tiny republic in what used to be Yugoslavia that remained as Serbia's only ally during the Balkan War that began in 1991—the father is not supposed to talk or smile at his child, or even look at him or her before the child talks or walks. The father's authority is unquestioned. "The father has the right to do anything he pleases with his son, even if the son is guilty of no offense" (1948b:23). This relationship leads to a "reaction formation" in which younger generations tend to adopt a philosophy of life completely contrary to that of their parents.

A comparison of social indicators and health statistics between Eastern and Western Europe suggests that Tomašić is at least on the right track. Eastern European rates of suicide are much higher than in Western Europe and the United States and may be characterized as being more fatalistic and altruistic, in Durkheim's (1897) vocabulary, compared with the predominantly egoistic and anomic types of suicide in the West. Compared with the Western European, the Eastern European smokes much more, dies sooner, suffers from much higher rates of infant mortality and cardiovascular disease, is more often a chronic alcoholic, is less satisfied with life and work, and suffers from higher rates of mental illness (see Eberstadt 1990; Nelson 1990; Skrbić et al. 1984). Medical sociologists have taught us that these medical problems are often linked to stressful social and personality conditions. Some observers have already invoked these facts to indict the failure of Communism and defend so-called decadent capitalism, but Tomašić's analysis suggests that the real culprit may be a disorganized personality structure or type of social character that preceded Communism. Careful scientific analysis would have to be conducted to establish this as a fact. Here, we are merely suggesting a hypothesis that seems plausible.

For his own empirical support, Tomašić analyzes Slavic popular culture and children's stories that tend to tell of a father's favoritism toward an obedient son. Disfavored children commonly develop emotional problems, and Tomašić refers to father-son conflicts in Dostoevsky's, Tolstoi's, and Gogol's novels as collective representations of these commonly experienced problems. Indeed, rereading Dostoevsky's *Brothers Karamazov* in this sociological context, not as a piece of great literature but as a cultural artifact, can be very illuminating. This masterpiece of Slavic literature is about three sons who wish to kill their father. There is no American equivalent of a literary classic that is this extremely Oedipal.

In general, Tomašić points to cultural indicators of extreme "lack of proportion in suffering as well as in pleasure" (1948b:24). He argues that "the lack of emotional balance may explain why the Dinaric warriors are more successful and efficient as guerrilla fighters than as regular army soldiers" (p. 31). It is interesting that the Balkan War that began in 1991 quickly degenerated into guerrilla warfare tactics as opposed to the more modernist, organized form of "civil war" one thinks of in the United States and the West. In fact, the Balkan War that began in 1991 was fought by "Serbian irregular troops" alongside the Serbian-dominated "Federal Army" against civilians and civilian militias. By modernist standards, the Serbian army's behavior should be called a coup d'état, because the Yugoslav president of the presidency, Stipe Mesić, was ignored when he tried to implement his constitutional right to govern the armed forces. But again, this sort of disorganized warfare is nothing new to the Balkans. It is habitual.

The poetry, popular lore, and art surrounding Prince Marko, the epic hero of the Balkans who lost the decisive battle to the Turks at Kosovo in 1389, is saturated with Oedipal themes and conflicts. In her *Prince Marko: The Hero of South Slavic Epics*, Tatyana Popović (1988) illustrates many of Tomašić's claims (without citing him) through her careful analysis of the brutality, hatred, and truly excessive violence found in the epics that commemorate Prince Marko. According to Tomašić, "The unbalanced temper of the heroes is strongly stressed in much of the oral poetry; Prince Marko is an extreme case of emotional instability" (1948b:33). The celebrated Yugoslav sculptor Ivan Meštrović burst onto the world's art scene in 1905 with his memorial to Prince Marko and this battle, which may be regarded as the Alamo of the Slavic people. It is significant that Prince Marko and most other national heroes in Yugoslavia are consistently portrayed as sitting on heroic horses which capture more attention than their human riders. Tomašić explains that the horse became man's best friend, a being that the Slavic warrior would trust more than his fellow humans. Freud would note that the horse symbolizes the father. Thus, the very symbolism used to represent historical Slavic heroism seems to signify some of the ambivalence, suspiciousness, and Oedipal conflict that Tomašić describes.

Also, it is worth noting that contemporary Kosovo is the site of human rights abuses by the Serbs against the majority Albanian population (Helsinki Watch 1990). The Serbian effort to cleanse their "sacred" grounds of Albanians seems to illustrate many of Tomašić's claims. It is remarkable that the United States and Western Europe have been tardy in responding to the plight of the Albanians in Kosovo in comparison with their sustained response to apartheid in South Africa, the Iraqi invasion of Kuwait, and other human rights abuses in the contemporary world.

Consider that Tito (as well as most other East European political leaders) ruled as a kind of Slavic father-figure. Those who obeyed him were rewarded, and dissenters were punished harshly, if not banished. But long after his death, Tito came to be embroiled in a controversy that seems unbelievable by modernist standards. The press coming out of Belgrade claimed that Tito was not a true Yugoslav because he was born in Croatia and because he gave the now-troubling Kosovo region its autonomy. Serbian crowds demanded that his body be removed from his grave in Belgrade. His image nevertheless remained powerful long after his death, and long after the fall of Communism even in non-Serbian regions of Yugoslavia in 1989. In Tomašić's scheme of things, he symbolized the tyrannical Slavic father, against whom one rebels even when he is dead or feeble. One can find many other such authoritarian father figures in Eastern Europe and the former USSR, from Ceauşescu in Romania before the revolution in 1989, to Gorbachev, who survived a coup attempt in August of 1991.

In sociological terms, the representation of Tito gave rise to an ambivalent, violent, symbolic "killing of the father" that coincided with the fall of Yugoslav Communism at the same time that his mythical qualities of being an authoritarian father persisted. The drama surrounding the rebellion against the fatherlike Tito is as engrossing and complex as Dostoevsky's portrait of the desire by Fyodor Pavlovich Karamazov's children to kill him. It is worth noting that, by contrast, Horkheimer and Adorno (1972) argue in their analysis of the rise of German fascism that Hitler was never a father figure to the German people.

Tomašić gives the compelling illustration that "the old slogan, for God, the King, and the country, is replaced by the slogan, for Tito and the Republic, and in the officially guided propaganda Tito is represented as an omnipotent, omniscient, and all-loving father of his people" (1948b:217). Indeed, despite the democratic reforms that have already occurred in former Yugoslavia (most notably in Slovenia and Croatia), and despite the reaction-formation against Tito, photographs of him—in seemingly countless poses, all equally unfriendly and austere—still adorned most public rooms in the country as late as 1991, as they did during the height of his power. We inquired of several bureaucrats in Croatia why they kept Tito's photographs on the walls of their offices, despite the democratic reforms, and received the reply that it was habit, or we received no reply at all. People did not seem to have a conscious reason for their attachment to the myth of Tito.

By contrast, American attitudes toward fathers, actual and symbolic, seem to be quite different. From David Riesman's study of other-directedness (1950) to contemporary studies of the family, the American father and mother are depicted as cultural objects that the child manipulates to get what he or she wants. In the American collective consciousness, which is predominantly democratic and egalitarian—if one is to believe Tocqueville and his successors, including Riesman and Bellah—there is no room for an authoritarian father figure. Presidents Reagan and Bush tried to come across as friends, communicators, or neighbors, and something of this kind has been occurring at least since FDR's fireside chats. As predicted by Tocqueville, American egalitarianism and sense of equality in the family create habits of the heart that inform political attitudes toward leaders.

Emotional Instability in the Quest for Success

Americans and Western Europeans take for granted that they display a certain amount of rationality and self-control, even in their immoderate, anomic tendencies toward hedonistic pleasure and consumerism (see Baudrillard 1986 and Lasch 1991). For example, leisure is tightly organized in the West and is run as a business (Rojek 1985). Tomašić exposes the searing contrast that there exists among the Dinaric and Ural Slavs a lack of proportion in suffering as well as pleasure, hope and despair, in all spheres of social life.

For example, Tomašić argues that cunning is regarded as astuteness of high order among the Dinaric Slavs. Whoever is able to defraud public institutions or women is regarded highly. There exists the general belief that "everybody is false as long as he can get away with it" (1948b:40). Hence, an inclination to spy upon other people is developed, and the notion of a secret police seems almost a natural outgrowth of this tendency. It is common for contemporary Yugoslavs in all walks of life to remark that "everybody is dirty," tainted, and stained by deceit, fraud, and theft, even after the peaceful transition to democracy in Croatia and Slovenia. It is easy to attribute this cynicism and guilt to the effects of Communism, a regime that thrived on deceit. But Tomašić's point seems to be that cunning and deceit, as character traits, preceded Communism. Again, even if it is true that Americans and Western Europeans are becoming increasingly cynical toward their social institutions (Bellah et al. 1991), it would be important to compare and contrast this cynicism that stems from modernity with the cynicism described by Tomašić.

Thus, the Western reactions to Serbian deceit vis-à-vis the Balkan War that began in 1991 betray a typically Western faith in contracts and the honor of keeping one's word, as well as a naïveté in dealing with a type of social character for whom deceit is automatic. For example, as of this writing in 1993, the West had brokered forty separate cease-fires in the Balkans, and each one was broken. The media reported over one thousand violations of the longest-lasting cease-fire, which began in December of 1991 and was supposed to lead to the introduction of peace-keeping troops. The Serbian government agreed that the United Nations should send in peace-keeping troops once a cease-fire was secured. But what Cyrus Vance, Lord Carrington, and other Western politicians could not see was the obvious motivation for the Serbs to make sure that peace is never achieved. If the cease-fires were always broken, then the peace-keeping troops would not be sent in, and the Serbian government could persist in its propaganda that it sought peace, even at the same time that it continued to seize territory. These are tactics that the Communist government (which was also dominated by Serbs) had perfected but that continued to work on the more honest and therefore gullible Western mind.

Again, we do not mean to imply that the West has not had its share of fraud, cunning, scandals, and deceit. We deny only that these traits are as typical in the West. On the contrary, we agree with Habermas in this regard that the ground or referent for communicative social action in the West is trust and honesty (for recent discussions, see Braaten 1991 and Holub 1991). And we are claiming that the Serbian government's actions in the war that began in 1991 illustrate Tomašić's argument that for the Dinaric social character, fraud and deceit are habitual. Moreover, these habits lead to a state of nearly chronic warfare.

American businesses attempting to open franchises in Eastern Europe find that it is difficult to get Slavs to smile at customers and imitate the friendly American "Hello, may I help you?" Eastern European customers and patrons are far more likely to scowl at each other during business transactions. There can be little doubt that the tyrannies of Eastern Europe were undercut by Western mass communications and the image of the happy, always-smiling luxurious West with its ample consumer goods, for which one does not have to stand in line. The Iron Curtain could not keep out the airways that brought in the Western smile. But the habitual lack of a smile in Eastern Europe is an important indicator that casual friendliness and trust among strangers are not taken for granted.

Examples of an unstable, impulsive work ethic in Eastern Europe and the USSR abound. Business meetings in former Yugoslavia are still likely to entail the consumption of large quantities of heavy liquor, even early in the morning. This practice is so common that it constitutes a cultural habit. Even psychiatrists and other mental health workers, who are often engaged in trying to cure the alcoholism that is the scourge of Eastern Europe and the USSR, frequently indulge in this barbaric custom of offering visitors hard liquor instead of coffee in the morning. It is significant to note, in this regard, that Acting President Gennady Yanayev, who led the coup against Gorbachev in 1991, was found drunk from vodka when he was finally arrested. In fact, his coconspirators were so entwined in booze, lies, and distrust that the *Wall Street Journal* dubbed their coup "the Vodka Putsch" (Gumbel 1991). The important point is that alcoholism has been and continues to be a significant and stereotypical social problem in Eastern Europe and the former USSR that may reflect the immoderation in social character that concerned Tomašić.

Balkan bus drivers are likely to interrupt a scheduled trip and route with a long stop at a tavern. Several cultural purposes are met by such interruptions in business routines simultaneously: machismo values are reinforced, a Byzantine spontaneity is exhibited as a kind of rebellion at the authority that tries to impose a rational work ethic, and a self-defeating dissipation is intertwined with wholesome values. So many Western visitors to the Balkans have experienced problems in what are considered normal, routine business dealings from Max Weber's ([1904] 1958) perspective that Slavic countries tend to be regarded as only a step above developing countries. The important point to consider is that to change Eastern European business habits into those of the successful West, one may have

to change the institutional and cultural structures that produce personality traits that cause these problems. Gorbachev recognized this
connection to some extent, because he made the war against alcoholism an integral part of his perestroika.

The cultural psychoanalyst C. G. Schoenfeld (1984) reminds
us that addiction to intoxicants may be regarded as a substitute for
therapy, or as a sort of poor man's psychotherapy. This is because
intoxicants relax the superego's control mechanisms, and especially
the faculty of guilt, and allow the alcoholic some catharsis of repressed impulses. Veblen (1899) captures another dimension of intoxication considered as a cultural problem (i.e., when it is a habitual mode of relating) when he argues that the addict conveys
prestige through his or her habitual intoxication, as if to say to the
world, "I can afford to waste my time and money in this dissipated
fashion." Both perspectives—the one emphasizing guilt and the other
prestige—nevertheless hold affinities with Tomašić's analysis and
deepen our understanding of deviance as a lived, concrete experience that varies from culture to culture. This is because repressed
guilt and the derivation of prestige from dissipation indicate severe
deviations from normal psychosocial development.

Several generations of post-Calvinist capitalists do not really
question the Western cultural myth that the God who is served by
the Protestant work ethic is good and just. Americans, in particular, exhibit this happy confidence in a just God to an extreme degree. No doubt this fact, among many others, led Robert N. Bellah
(1967) to conceive the concept of American civil religion as a phenomenon that is separate from bona fide religion but that takes as
its basic premise that America is a nation that puts its faith in God
and is in turn blessed by God. But Tomašić notes that the Slavs do
not picture God as just, merciful, and benevolent, but rather as ar-
bitrary and cruel, "to whom they sometimes refer as that old bloody
slayer" (1948b:42). God himself is cursed in daily language, to an
extreme degree, along with all the angels and saints. This is still
true in contemporary Yugoslavia. One commonly hears the expression "God be f——d" and other blasphemous swearing at all levels

of social class and without any regard for the presence of children or women.

While most of Europe is less Puritanical than the United States with regard to the public display of nudity, Yugoslavs carry this openness too far. Schoolchildren wait to catch buses and trams next to kiosks that display not only nudity but pornography. In general, post-Communism has meant the sudden and widespread proliferation of pornography in Eastern Europe and the former USSR. Despite the great premium placed on motherhood, norms of respect for women, and even the Communist "liberation" of women, Tomašić's observation still applies that in backward Dinaric regions, the primary function of women is the bearing of male children and, next to this, the performance of physical labor. In some mountainous regions of Serbia and Montenegro, it is still the custom that women must not eat at the same table as men. Even in the 1990s, one will find Yugoslav women plowing the fields while the men rest, drink coffee, and gossip. Journalists commonly express shock at this state of affairs (cf. Danforth 1990), but it is more difficult to establish the proportion of these unequal family arrangements to the democratic arrangements, which certainly exist as well.

From the perspective developed by Norbert Elias (1982) and others that civilized behavior entails certain restraints on bodily impulses and expressions regarded as disgusting, crude, and exploitative, one would have to conclude that much daily speech and social intercourse in Slavic lands is still barbaric—especially in the mountainous regions. For example, Elias concentrates on the public control of spitting, coughing, passing gas, belching, nudity, scratching one's genitals, and other bodily phenomena that modern people have come to define as disgusting. Our contention that Slavs are less civilized according to these criteria set forth by Elias is not intended to belittle Slavic culture. But it does raise the question: If bodily functions are inadequately constrained in Eastern Europe, by Western standards, why would one suppose that other impulses—including violent ones—would be any more restrained? The more important point is that neither in the past nor currently has savage violence been constrained adequately in the Balkans. Tomašić (1953:117) writes that "the Russian heart is infinitely pitiful and tender, but at the same time what gross and often completely aimless cruelty and tyranny are to be found in Russian life." He quotes Tolstoi to the effect that there exist two Russias, one rooted in universal culture and ideas of goodness, honor, and freedom, while the other is "the Russia of the dark forests, the animal Russia, the fanatic Russia, the Mongol-Tartar Russia," Russia as the negation of Europe (p. 119). Anyone who examines the details of day-to-day social interaction in any Eastern European nation is likely to conclude that Tolstoi's observation can be extended and still applies to some extent. For example, the war that began in 1991 in former Yugoslavia exhibited fantastic barbarism, including the mutilation and torture of prisoners before and after execution; attacks on schools, churches, and hospitals; and the acceptance of violence against civilians as commonplace, acts that are regarded as war crimes in the West. Milovan Djilas and other survivors of World War II have written many accounts of similar barbarism. Even if one wants to contend that Americans and Western Europeans have committed atrocities during wars as well, it is generally accepted that in keeping with the modernist agenda, the West rationalizes, attempts to control, and systematizes its violent propensities (see Bauman 1991, among many others). In stark contrast, the Yugoslav War that began in 1991 and previous Balkan wars exhibited violence that might be regarded as criminal, gratuitous, and nonrational from an instrumental perspective. For example, there is no rational explanation for the Serbs' destroying Dubrovnik, Vukovar, Sarajevo, Gorazde, and other cities even as they claimed that these cities were being liberated.

The Problem of Guilt

Eastern Europeans, who eagerly watch Hollywood films, frequently remark that for them it is amazing that American movie stars hardly ever betray any guilt in their films. Slavs are bewildered by the typical American lines "Don't worry about it" or "You don't have to feel bad." Indeed, the year 1989 closed and 1990 began to the tune of the American hit song "Don't Worry, Be Happy." In stark contrast to the seemingly guilt-free American, guilt is thoroughly woven into the cultural fabric of Eastern Europe, and especially the regions of what used to be Yugoslavia. It has been kept alive by both the churches and Communism, but ultimately it can be traced to the Oedipal conflicts uncovered by Tomašić. Authoritarianism in the family as well as in politics is sustained by and gives rise to the phenomenon of guilt. Freud examined this phenomenon in the context of turn-of-the-century inner-directedness, and it still seems applicable to Eastern European social character.

Tomašić found that the sense of guilt was extremely developed in Russia at the turn of the century and that it is a theme developed extensively by Dostoevsky, Tolstoi, and other great Slavic novelists. But guilt dominates contemporary Slavic novels and films as well. Tomašić remarks that a common expression in Slavic social interaction is *oprosti,* "forgive me," and that the same sentiment is manifested in the readiness to shed tears at the slightest provocation. This is still true in former Yugoslavia. The expression *oprosti* is so common that one uses it whenever one disagrees with someone else in the most mundane conversations—as if the collective quantity of guilt is so great that it must be expiated almost constantly. There is no real equivalent in the United States. The comedian Steve Martin could mock the expression "excuse me" in his comedy routines precisely because it has lost its cultural punch in the West.

Additionally, guilt is used by Dinaric Slavs in the media as a political weapon, as various ethnic groups rake up evils from the past to make other groups feel guilty. Thus, for all the decades that followed Tito's rise to power, the Serbs brought up the Ustaše atrocities from World War II in a systematic and sustained effort to make the Croatians feels guilty. (Ustaše refers to a Nazi puppet government that was set up in Croatia by Ante Pavelić.) By contrast, even if some Croatians retorted by holding up to the Serbs their Nazi collaboration (Cohen 1992) and other atrocities from World War II, their propaganda machine was never as organized or sustained as the one orchestrated by the Serbs. This is because the Serbs managed to convince the West that its attacks on Croatia and Bosnia-Hercegovina were justified with reference to atrocities that had been committed fifty years ago. At the negotiating table, Croatia's and Bosnia-Hercegovina's quests for independence and Serbia's unjustified aggression against them were put on an equal footing.

Obviously, all parties that were involved in World War II are guilty of some sort of atrocity or crime against humanity. This applies even to the United States when one considers its merciless bombing of Dresden, Hiroshima, and Nagasaki, among others. For example, this point was brought home momentarily by President Bush's refusal in December of 1991 to apologize on behalf of the United States for its dropping the atomic bomb on Japan. The former East and West Germanies debated whether they should feel guilty for Nazism, fascism, the Holocaust, or Communism, and who should apologize for what. Gorbachev finally apologized for the lies and atrocities committed by Stalin. But the important point is that this finger-pointing and attributing of guilt seems to be very pronounced in Slavic lands; that it is a startling tactic, when one considers that all sides are objectively guilty of something, and when compared with the truly more guilt-free American cultural pattern; and that most countries that were involved in World War II have managed to bury past animosities and move on with the modernity project. But not Serbia, which in the 1980s and 1990s relives the wrongs committed against it as if they occurred yesterday, and which is not willing to admit its own share of collective guilt.

The contrast with the West is worth considering. American children are brought up not to feel guilty, perhaps even when they should. In fact, they are admonished to feel good about themselves, to hold a positive self-image, and not to dwell on mistakes. In contrast to the East Europeans, Americans do not, as a rule, dwell upon their collective role or guilt in the wrongful imprisonment of Japanese Americans and Eskimos during World War II, dropping the atom bomb, Vietnam, the massacre of retreating troops during the 1991 war with Iraq, or the fact that innocent people were killed during the 1990 invasion of Panama, among many other events that might be used to provoke guilt. By contrast, any newspaper or magazine in Serbia routinely contains statements of blame against the Vatican, the Kremlin, the United States, the Turks, the former Austro-Hungarian Empire, the foreign press, and especially neighboring ethnic groups, among many others, for faults real or imagined.

The objectivity of the claims that are put forth is not the important point to consider, given that all parties involved share some objective reasons for guilt. What is more important, for the purposes of the present analysis, is the cultural proclivity to use guilt as a weapon, to draw on the importance and centrality of guilt in the Dinaric social character in making assessments of the world.

Consider that in the United States the state of Texas is known to be responsible for a great deal of the money wasted in the savings and loan scandal. The rest of the United States will have to bail out the troubled banks, especially the ones in Texas. Yet, despite some complaints, one does not find that Texas has been singled out in any sort of organized guilt campaign. Were Texas located in the Balkans, one would almost certainly find that neighboring nations, even republics within nations, would impose sanctions of all sorts as punishment for its collective guilt. For example, in 1989 Serbia imposed economic sanctions against Slovenia for its refusal to allow a group of Serbs to demonstrate in Ljubljana. Moscow's imposition of sanctions against Lithuania in 1990 is well known, but such acts are common in Eastern Europe, even if most of them are not covered in the Western media. A primitive notion of collective guilt, treated at length by Durkheim's follower Paul Fauconnet

(1920) and virtually unknown in the West, still animates much of Eastern Europe's political life.

Implications

The negative aspects of the Slavic personality structure may have to be self-consciously changed in order to put into place free-market and democratic forces as they are known in the West. Of course, these so-called negative aspects (emotional instability, authoritarianism, and so on) are such only in relation to the Western model of modernity that has dominated the world since the last century. Such a change would be difficult, for it would entail a revolution in habits of the heart that was achieved by the Puritans hundreds of years ago. Even if such a cultural revolution could occur, it would probably produce decadent, anomic, and other negative aspects of Western Enlightenment.

There is no good reason to suppose that the Eastern Europeans might not find their own, unique road to modernity, as illustrated by the Japanese experiment in modernization. Although the possibility exists that they shall find a softer, more compassionate brand of socialism or hybrid form of capitalism in tune with a mother-centered culture and cult of Mary, there also exists the real danger that the traditional, authoritarian, unstable habits of the heart will reassert themselves again. In fact, Erich Fromm's (1962) observation that machismo values develop as a reaction against mother-centeredness, and vice versa, needs to be reexamined in the Eastern European context. Fromm's psychoanalytic sociology complements Tomašić's approach.

Tomašić fears that in Eastern Europe the powerful are admired even if they are unjust, and those who rebel at previous systems of authority eventually, unconsciously, repeat the previous authoritarian patterns. With regard to the Communist takeover of power, Tomašić writes that "the ascending group was interested only in taking the place of those whom they overthrew, not in effecting any radical social alternations, so that Dinaric society did not change fundamentally for a number of centuries." In Yugoslavia, the Partisans showed this tendency in their rebellion against the old aristocracy; the Bolsheviks established a messianic dictatorship every bit as total as the previous systems of power imposed by the Czars and the Russian Orthodox church; and by implication, *some* contemporary rebellions against Communism may exhibit similar tendencies. Tomašić gives the illustration that, "not unlike their Ural-Altaic predecessors and the bandit heroes [of the past], the Partisan communist rulers of Eastern European countries also take personal advantage of their political power. They appropriate for their own use other people's property. They live in luxurious palaces, are surrounded by many servants and courtiers, indulge in publicly displaying their wealth and position." Some have observed that this pattern is already being repeated by the new, purportedly democratic rulers in much of Eastern Europe.

Tomašić attributes this repetition of old evils to a family structure that fosters emotional instability and extreme ambivalence: "Thus we find the urge for destruction and identification with suffering as fundamental aspects of the ideology of Russian revolutionary movements." As contemporary illustrations of this fundamental, Slavic ambivalence, consider that in March of 1990 newly elected President Iliescu of Romania called on the country's coal miners to suppress brutally those who opposed his methods. The previous dictator, Ceaușescu, had been overthrown for only a few months when reports of old dictatorial habits began to appear. A month later, reports emerged that Lech Walesa in Poland was abandoned politically by his own allies for displaying authoritarianism. Walesa had been hailed as a hero in the West for sustaining the Solidarity movement, but Tomašić's analysis leads one to suspect that Walesa may have rebelled at the previous authoritarianism only to establish his own. Yeltsin, Tudjman, Havel, and other democratically elected leaders have also been accused of reverting to autocratic habits. Contemporary opposition parties throughout Eastern

Europe routinely accuse the newly elected "democratic" regimes of behaving as the former Bolshevik regimes did.

The remarkable thing about most democratic elections in Eastern Europe in 1990 has been the nearly complete mandate given to the leaders and the lack of an effective opposition. In these and other ways, some Eastern European leaders are already exhibiting a drive toward total power, intolerance for dissent, censorship, and willingness to resort to the brutality that Tomašić claims are essential parts of the Dinaric mentality regarding power. Most of those who were elected to power in Eastern Europe were former Communists, so that the danger of a circulating elite seems very real. The possibility exists that former undemocratic policies will persist in new guises. The old system may reemerge because the same people and the same habits operate, which leads to secrecy, terror, and tyranny.

The most common and naive response to the events in Eastern Europe is the simple belief that although they may face some rough periods in their quest for democracy, Eastern Europeans will ultimately succeed in adopting Western-style free enterprise and democracy. The dark possibility that old forms of totalitarianism may reemerge is usually dismissed as pessimism. Such naive optimism is hardly questioned in the West. As of this writing, it is unfashionable to refer to "social character," although Tocqueville, Riesman, and Bellah are admired for their efforts in describing the American social character. A significant contradiction in these postmodern times is that we want to believe that human nature is essentially universal and that history has come to an end, even as most Americans and Western Europeans are wary of the changes occurring in Eastern Europe.

The reluctance to refer to anything like a permanent personality or social structure is part of the long-standing crisis within the Western social sciences that stems from extreme cultural and moral relativism. Nevertheless, it seems more reasonable to agree with the classical founding fathers of sociology and to suppose that within specific cultural contexts, certain personality and social structures will be relatively fixed and permanent. The possibility of engaging in social research rests on this assumption, and it is an assumption that rests on mountains of empirical research. The extreme antistructuralist view is a kind of epistemological nihilism, or at best it assumes the kind of plasticity and malleability to "human nature" that Marxists have assumed. The failure of Marxist ideology in Communist countries suggests that this assumption needs to be questioned within the social sciences as well.

From the cultural perspective adopted in this book, it is incredible that Communism did not succeed in brainwashing the majority of the populations it ruled, because politicians and laypersons in America in the postwar years routinely assumed that it would (Riesman 1954). Equally incredible is the fact that the indigenous culture of these nations was able to resist the ideology of Communism. Thus, some sort of underlying structure apparently did survive surface changes, and this structure can be discussed objectively and scientifically without succumbing to the essentialist assumptions that are criticized by some social scientists.

This underlying cultural structure is emerging with extraordinary force following the repression of national and other cultural identities that had been enforced by the Communists. These include the gentle and positive as well as the brutal and negative habits of the heart. Ancient ethnic conflicts and animosities are so strong that some have degenerated into racism. While Americans celebrated Halloween in 1990 as a "fun" holiday, most Croatian Catholics visited the graves of their ancestors amid flowers and candles in a ritual that can be likened to primitive ancestor worship (see Hertz [1907–1909] 1960). Street names are being changed back to their pre-Communist names. Nationalist songs, old monuments, and even pre-Communist vocabularies are being restored and revived. The dominant Balkan response to liberation from Communism has been to retreat into past traditions, not to embrace Western institutions wholeheartedly.

It was a mistake for Westerners to assume that Communism could obliterate native Eastern European culture. But it is equally incorrect to assume that free enterprise and liberal democracy will automatically replace Communism in Eastern Europe. This is the mistake made by Fukuyama (1992) and his followers who promulgate the "end of history" thesis. One really must consider the irony that Fukuyama and the Bolsheviks use the same slogan (end of history), draw on the same philosophers (Hegel and Marx), and hold to the same, arrogant assumptions concerning social engineering. Eastern Europe, however, has its own complex culture, still poorly understood by its own citizens as well as by observers in the rest of the world.

Even though there appears to exist a superficial similarity between our argument and that in the works by Hannah Arendt (1962), Theodor Adorno (1950), Max Horkheimer (1972), and the rest of the Frankfurt School on authoritarianism, we are attempting a different explanation in our effort to draw upon Tomašić in the context of classical sociology. Contextually, most critical theorists and theorists of mass society were Marxist in orientation, and their work bespeaks the ideological slant of examining authoritarianism as a fascist phenomenon derived from the Englightenment. Our aim is different: to expose the commensurability of a kind of authoritarianism with Marxist ideology and, more significantly, a non-Enlightenment-based cultural proclivity toward totalitarianism that preceded Marxism.

4. Veblen and Spengler on Barbarism within Modernity

Given the controversial nature of cultural analysis in the contemporary sociological setting, we hesitate to proceed further with an analysis of Slavic social character without further elaboration. The notion of social character is as foreign sounding to most contemporary English-speaking readers as the new names of nations that have emerged in the post-Communist landscape. We propose to develop the central focus of this book cautiously, by reviewing previous, exemplary efforts to comprehend the *cultural* origins of World War I by Thorstein Veblen (1915) and Oswald Spengler (1926). If World War I signaled the collapse of culture in a manner that shocked and frightened intellectuals at the previous turn of the century, it may well be the case that the collapse of Communism at the present turn of the century signifies more than an opportunity for capitalist expansion. We return to Veblen and Spengler in order to gain a context and perspective on Tomašić's theoretical assessment of the cultural origins of instability in the Balkans.

Veblen and Spengler are as unknown to most English-speaking readers as the names Croatia and Slovenia. But we have been implying all along that the collapse of Communism signals a wider collapse of modernist assessments (Bauman 1992). Veblen and Spengler emerge from the ruins of contemporary sociology as much as Croatia and Slovenia emerged from the ruins of Communism — both modern sociology and Communism assumed that social order could be achieved through social engineering and that it would lead to progress. Veblen and Spengler are among the many classical thinkers from the previous turn of the century who questioned these naive assumptions. We turn to them because they can still teach us much about the present crisis. By citing them, we can demonstrate that Tomašić was writing in an intellectual context that had been established by them as well as by others harking back to Tocqueville.

A final reason for referring to Veblen and Spengler is that they offer a corrective to Hegel's (1899) notion of the end of history which has inspired Fukuyama's (1992) now-famous revival of that same concept. But Fukuyama omits—somewhat conveniently, it seems—the notion that Hegel thought that Germany would achieve the end of history while the rest of the world, including America, would remain mired in it. Moreover, it is difficult, if not impossible, to derive the individualism and liberal democracy that is so dear to Americans from Hegel's philosophy, because Hegel enshrined the strong, even despotic German state (Ryan 1992). For the sake of approaching an objective appraisal, it is important to contrast Veblen's and Spengler's pessimistic assessments of both history and Germany's role in it with Hegel's and Fukuyama's optimistic appraisals. Finally, we suggest that German imperialism in the twentieth century might be instructive to students of Serbian and other Slavic forms of imperialism as the century draws to a close.

Veblen on the Barbaric Temperament

Two books by Thorstein Veblen are especially important to our argument here, namely, *Imperial Germany and the Industrial Revolution* (1915) and *An Inquiry into the Nature of Peace and the Terms of Its Perpetuation* (1917). They are important because, in these books, Veblen foreshadows Tomašić's argument that aggressive nationalism is not a biological proclivity derived from human nature but, rather, is a cultural habit derived from human "second nature." In particular, Veblen argued that imperial Germany (as well as imperial Japan) possessed barbaric "habits of the fight" that were handed down by tradition and that did not disappear simply because of modernity and its more peaceable values.

One of Veblen's most profound insights is that barbarism can coexist with a modern mind-set. David Riesman (1953) remains one of the most important thinkers who appreciate Veblen. According to Riesman (1964:391), "To view modern civilization as still barbaric at its core seems less funny today than to those who laughed in 1899 (at the end of the splendid little war with Spain) at *The Theory of the Leisure Class*." Perhaps Veblen's theory is still less funny as the present century draws to a close, a time that is witnessing the resurgence of barbarism, despite modernity and the best-laid plans for the end of history.

At the turn of the previous century, Germany embarked on a massive program to catch up with England with regard to industrialization and overall modernization, but it did not shed its cultural proclivity toward barbarism. Instead, there resulted a condition that Veblen termed "cultural lag," according to which Germany became a powerful, industrial, military nation but nevertheless retained a social character that was still aggressive and backward. This unhappy wedding of modern habits pertaining to efficiency and barbaric habits of the fight led inevitably, according to Veblen, to Germany's well-known role in both world wars. Riesman (1953) is correct to cite Veblen as the only accurate prognosticator of these two important events.

Our aim in exploring Veblen's argument in further detail here is to make the connection that a similar state of cultural lag may have occurred in Serbia and also in other nations that used to be ruled by Communism. To the extent that Communism is a child of the Enlightenment and sought to modernize the nations it ruled in an effort to "win" the race with the bourgeois, capitalist West, it certainly achieved some modernist goals (even if Brzezinski and others are correct that it fell rapidly behind the West). But our focus is on the mentality of a people, its habits as enshrined in its culture. Many formerly Communist nations are every bit as belligerent and barbaric as they were before the onset of Communism, the only difference being that they are now better armed and equipped to carry out their belligerent aims. For the sake of clarity, it is important to cite a possible source of conceptual confusion when analyzing Veblen. It has to do with his own habit of inventing various "instincts" and "habits" that do not seem to correspond neatly with the rest of his conceptual edifice. Thus, he refers variously to habits of the mind, habits of the fight, habits of the heart, habits of thought, or just plain habits. Similarly, he refers to the instinct of workmanship, the parenting instinct, barbaric instincts, and so on. Riesman (1953) is probably correct that Veblen did not mean to imply that his use of "instincts" resembles in any way the biological understanding of what constitutes an instinct. Rather, and much like Freud and other theorists from the previous fin de siècle, Veblen invented all sorts of "instincts" and "habits" as part of his conceptual apparatus, but always in the cultural context that we have already discussed. Moreover, he may have preferred the phrase "habits of the mind" when referring to modern culture in order to differentiate modernity from the gemeinschaft context, in which habits of the heart are important. The essential thing to keep in mind is that Veblen was a pioneer of the cultural approach that we have traced from Tocqueville to Tomašić and Bellah and that we are returning to Veblen in order to make better sense of the present.

One more contextual point is in order. Riesman (1964:395) asks the rhetorical question: "Before the [Great] war, Veblen plainly regarded American capitalists as latter day barbarians; how is it that he suddenly sees the Germans as the real barbarians?" Riesman never answers this question, although it is important. Our reply is that Veblen regarded all cultures as a mixture of barbaric and peaceable traits and that he apparently arrived at the conclusion that America would become more peaceable compared with Germany and Japan. Looking back over the previous century as a whole, one has to conclude that overall, Veblen's assessment was correct.

Veblen ([1915] 1964:238) argues that the German culture that laid the groundwork for both world wars was out of touch with neighboring cultures as well as with portions of its own culture:

> What the Fatherland has to offer in this way is, in its elements, out of date and therefore out of touch with the habits of thought in such communities of a maturer culture as, e.g., the French or the English; the chief distinctive characteristic of the German culture being a retarded adherence to certain medieval or submedieval habits of thought, the equivalents of which belong father back than the historical present in the experience of these others. It is further argued, on similar ground, that any endeavor to hold fast the main body of this peculiarly German culture *in statu quo* within the confines of the Fatherland would similarly be nugatory, because as a cultural scheme it is out of date and touch with itself, *in that it is in part archaic and in part quite new* [emphasis added].

Veblen is quick to add that "all this, of course, does not bear on the intrinsic merits of this body of culture or on the question of its desirability." What it does mean is that German culture in Veblen's time existed in "an exceptionally unstable, transitory, and in a sense unripe phase." Furthermore, and because it comprised "certain archaic elements—as, e.g., its traditional penchant for Romantic metaphysics and feudalistic loyalty—together with some of the latest ramifications of mechanistic science and an untempered application of the machine industry, it necessarily lacks that degree of homogeneity in its logic and orientation that would characterise a maturer cultural complex" (p. 239).

One could apply Veblen's insights to the current crisis in post-Communist lands and argue that many of them also constitute unstable compounds of modernity in an uneasy alliance with archaic, nationalist traits. Even if most political analysts do not know or cite Veblen, the expressed fears that nuclear weapons may get "into the wrong hands" e.g., (virulent nationalists) following the dissolution of the Soviet Union lend indirect credence to Veblen's theory.

Veblen also links the concept "territorial State" to the persistence of primitive habits of thought in a modern context. Specifically, he argues that had Germany been more thoroughly modern, it would have given rise to cultural habits that do not place credence on territory, for that is a throwback to feudal times. Instead, modern habits foster tendencies toward an international division of labor that opens up markets and that treats national boundaries as sorts of accidents, or conventions, that are not worth going to war over. In this sense, the dream of a United States of Europe and the European Community are modernist tendencies, whereas German imperialism was a barbaric throwback. But again, the more important point for the purposes of the present analysis is that in the Yugoslav War that began in 1991, Serbia used modern weapons and one of the largest armies in Europe in order to seize territory and expand its borders—in other words, for imperialist aims. In this regard, too, contemporary Serbia may be compared with historical, imperial Germany.

Veblen argues further that modernist habits or traditions stress civil liberties, whereas barbaric habits stress loyalty to one's superiors. Imperial Germany tried to combine these two contrary habits in an unhappy mix, according to Veblen (1917:112):

> So, the development and elaboration of these modern principles of civic liberty . . . under the hand of the German Intellectuals has uniformly run out into Pickwickian convolutions, greatly suggestive of a lost soul seeking a place to rest. . . . But at no point and in no case have either the proposals or their carrying out taken shape as a concrete application of the familiar principle of popular self-direction. It has always come to something in the way of a concessive or expedient mitigation of the antagonistic principle of personal authority. Where the forms of self-government or of individual self-direction have concessively been installed, under the Imperial rule, they have turned out to be an imitative structure with some shrewd provision for their coercion or inhibition at the discretion of an irresponsible authority.

One could easily make the connection that many newly elected, democratic governments in post-Communist lands are similarly imitating Western democracy while preserving many of the previously held autocratic habits. Veblen stresses that in these and other instances of cultural lag, one should not impugn the sound intelligence or the good faith of human agents trying to implement new habits into old cultural settings. Rather, one must realize that these are "circumstances over which they could have no control, since they were circumstances that shaped their own habits of thought, have placed it beyond their competence to apprehend or to formulate these alien principles (habits of thought) concretely in those alien institutional details and by the alien logic with which they could have no working acquaintance" (1917:113).

So what is one to do? If intelligence and good faith are not sufficient to overcome the power of habits—which, almost by definition, belie the power of the heart over the mind—then how does one change habits that are bellicose or violent? Veblen's unsatisfactory reply is that "the change of habituation" involves divesting a culture of previous habits and habituation to new ones. But who and what will direct this divestiture? Veblen does not seem to realize the dangerous implications of the social engineering that would be involved. The Bolsheviks, fascists, Nazis, and other extremists have given the twentieth century all the divestitures of negative habits that it can take.

Obviously, such a change "would not therefore come about abruptly or swiftly" because "institutional changes take time, being creations of habit" (p. 143). Veblen should be taken very seriously, when one considers that the bellicose habits he identified in imperial Germany were important factors in two world wars. The obvious connection to the current state of affairs in post-Communist lands is that if Veblen's analysis of the antecedents to the previous two world wars holds merit, then drastic changes toward democratic institutions should not be expected quickly.

Another dimension to Veblen's analysis is more subtle and needs to be emphasized more clearly. Strictly speaking, Veblen is not a typical Enlightenment thinker. He does not believe that the truth shall set an individual or an entire people free. Mere intellectual acumen, even if widespread, is not enough to civilize and pacify a bellicose culture. Rather, old undesirable habits must be self-consciously replaced with new desired habits, a task that is exceedingly difficult. There is some overlap here with Freud's therapeutic process, which also involves rational insight versus the unconscious powers derived from the id.[1] (For more on the connections between Freud and Veblen, see Schneider 1948.) For verification, one has only to consider the travail involved in changing private, obnoxious habits, such as smoking or eating fatty foods.

Thus, Veblen does not believe that modernity automatically leads to open-mindedness, tolerance, pluralism, or other aspects of social progress that one has grown accustomed to associating with the Enlightenment project. The gist of Veblen's critique is that in his day, "the German people have acquired the use of the modern industrial arts in the highest state of efficiency, at the same time that they have retained unabated the fanatical loyalty of feudal barbarism" (p. 201). The end result is that *the logic of warfare comes to be the same mechanistic logic that makes possible the modern state of industrial arts!* Nazi Germany, especially, displayed this tragic conjunction of barbarism and the "instinct for workmanship," but so have other modern nations, even if their level of barbarism as well as workmanship never equaled those of Germany.

Veblen exposes one to the reality of a culture working at cross-purposes with itself as well as with the democratic principles of respect for human rights that Tocqueville uncovered. Modernity is coupled with old-fashioned barbarism. The end result is a hybrid form of barbarism that is more deadly than previous forms precisely because it is more technologically advanced. In Veblen's (1917:314) words,

> The menace of warlike aggression from such dynastic States, e.g., as Imperial Germany and Imperial Japan is due to their having acquired a competent use of this modern technology, while they have not yet had time to lose that spirit of dynastic loyalty which they have carried over from an archaic order of things, out of which they have emerged at a very appreciably later period (last half of the nineteenth century) than those democratic peoples whose peace they now menace.

Likewise, one must confront the question whether the lands that used to be ruled by Communism have had a chance to emerge from their archaic, undemocratic habits. This question implies two related problems: Given that Communism attempted to brainwash whole peoples into an undemocratic, totalitarian culture, was it something new to the nations it conquered, or was it an extension of previously held undemocratic cultural pockets in those same nations? No single answer will encompass all of Eastern Europe and what used to be the Soviet Union. And the answer will not be simple, in any event. This entire book is geared toward an exploration of the factors involved in searching for a reply.

As stated previously, Croatia and Slovenia are undoubtedly more democratic in cultural outlook than are Serbia and Montenegro, for example. However, one could argue that Croatia and Slovenia are not as democratic as some other nations with an established democratic tradition. But given that the cultural conflict between the Croatians and Slovenes versus the Serbs and Montenegrins is old and well established, the new factors that must be taken into account are that (1) these old enemies are facing each other as a continuation of a long cultural conflict that preceded Communism and was not extinguished by it, and (2) they face each other with better technology than ever before, even if that technology is not up to par with that of the superpowers (or of contemporary Germany, Japan, and the European Community).

Moreover, the contemporary conflict in the Balkans serves as a laboratory for similar conflicts in the other post-Communist lands. For example, shortly after the dissolution of the Soviet Union, Russia and the Ukraine argued over who would control the military arsenal that technically belonged to the newly formed commonwealth. Thus, using Veblen, one has to fear for the possibility of extreme "cultural lag" in post-Communist lands and for the extreme possibility of a protracted and bloody struggle among cultures that sincerely seek peace in a modern context at the same time that they seek territory, power, and other barbaric goals. No doubt the idea of cultural lag is one of the most important in the sociological vocabulary and is useful in assessing the direction of post-Communist developments.

Reappreciating the Decline of the West

In a preface to his famous *Decline of the West* (first published in 1918), Oswald Spengler admits that he conceived this book in 1914 as a way of comprehending the First World War. Like Veblen, Spengler sought a cultural explanation for Germany's role in the war, as well as the roles of the other national actors. Like Veblen and the other fin-de-siècle thinkers we have been following, Spengler relied on an opposition similar to that between "heart" and "mind" that was made famous by Schopenhauer and Nietzsche. Spengler expressed this opposition as one between culture (heart) and civilization (mind). He felt that each of the world's great cultures (Arabic, Indian, Chinese, Greek, Roman, and Western) followed a unique path from culture to civilization but that in the end, the "late," or dying, stages of civilization have displayed certain similarities. One of the most important symptoms of the autumn stage of civilization is imperialism: "Imperialism is Civilization unadulterated. In this phenomenal form the destiny of the West is now irrevocably set" (Spengler [1926] 1961:36).

It is important to note that Spengler rejects the positivistic assumption that there exists a single world history, with the West at the pinnacle of progress and all other cultures that preceded it as being somehow backward or barbaric. Spengler was among the first to proclaim the doctrine of cultural relativism (widely accepted today), which holds, instead, that each culture has its own life span that progresses from barbaric to civilized. The new twist offered by Spengler, however, is that so-called civilized cultures often display a second version of barbarism that is often as violent, heartless, and cruel as any that one might like to attribute to our ancestors. Clearly, Veblen's (1899) analysis of barbaric habits of the fight that persist despite modernity is commensurate with Spengler's thesis.

From Spengler's point of view, one must get used to viewing the barbarian Genghis Khan as civilized, because he acted on the imperialistic, expansionist doctrine common to all late civilizations, on a par with the age of European and American imperialism at the turn of the previous century. As we shall see in the remainder of this book, this insight shall make an important difference in explaining the fall of Communism and its aftermath.

According to Spengler, the opposition between ancient Greek *soul* and Roman *intellect* is the difference between culture and civilization. Elsewhere, he referred to this antithesis as "Culture and Civilization—the living body of a soul and the mummy of it" (p. 353). Furthermore, he argued that it was the *destiny* of every culture to become civilization, which is to say, autumnal, artificial, rootless, "under forms fashioned by the intellect" (p. 353). "The transition from Culture to Civilization was accomplished for the Classical world in the fourth, for the Western in the nineteenth century," according to Spengler (p. 32). Spengler draws on Nietzsche, echoes Tönnies and other fin-de-siècle cultural sociologists, and influenced Arnold Toynbee to liken the West's place in history with the fall of the Roman Empire: "For the Classical world this condition [nihilism] sets in with the Roman age; for us it will set in from about the year 2000" (Spengler [1926] 1961:352).

For Spengler, late civilization is destined to become expansionist and imperialistic, unspiritual, barbaric, disciplined, and practical (p. 32). It will not feel like the end of culture to its citizens, yet its symptoms shall be unmistakably similar to that of the end of the Roman Empire. In this sense, World War I was preordained hundreds of years ago, according to Spengler (p. 47). The imperialism and expansionism associated with World War I do not have to be exclusively military. Spengler connects the notion of a United States of Europe to Napoleon and cites both as manifestations of the transition from culture to late civilization. This observation is still relevant, for the dream of a United States of Europe, which is based on economic imperialism, is taking shape in our lifetime. Elsewhere, he cites socialism as an "end-phenomenon" and as "civilization-ethics" (p. 361). This is because socialism tries to impose compassion as an imperative command, a Kantian categorical imperative valid for all, as a universal morality that must be *imposed on others by force.* In this sense, organized, systematized socialism is an expansionist doctrine compared with the message of tolerance and compassion espoused by Jesus Christ: "There is a hardness in the sort of compassion that was practised by the German mystics, the German and Spanish military Orders, the French and English Calvinists," and, one might add, the Bolsheviks (p. 350).

Spengler isolates *a sense of mission* as an integral aspect of civilization ethics. In this regard Communism may be regarded as a product of late civilization. There can be little doubt that the Bolsheviks portrayed Communism as a mission for messianic redemption of the suffering classes: "In this manner, the Bolsheviks have been able to appeal to supra-ethical and supra-personal loyalties and to all-human longings, not unlike a universal church" (Tomašić 1953:20). Similarly, Mao was fond of interpreting Marx to the effect that "to make an omelette, one must break a few eggs" (quoted in Harvey 1989:4). Spengler enables one to interpret Communism as a modernist product of late civilization—complete with messianic and other expansionist dimensions—that was transplanted onto predominantly Byzantine cultures that were themselves heading into the autumn of their cultural careers. "There are no Classical world-improvers," Spengler wrote (p. 342).

This interpretation dovetails with those made by Veblen as well as Tomašić; all three thinkers were able to isolate imperialist cultural habits and tendencies and, on the basis of this cardinal trait, predict tremendous instability, war, and eventual cultural self-destruction. True, both Veblen and Spengler were most concerned with imperial Germany, but their analyses lend themselves easily to the case of imperial Russia. Russia dominated the Communist Soviet Union and, in a sense, transformed its imperialist tendencies in name only. The commonwealth of former Soviet republics that was formed in 1991 also gave Russia and its president, Boris Yeltsin, more power and privilege than it did the other member states. Similarly, Serbia dominated the Communist Yugoslavia, so much so that following open and free elections in the early 1990s, only Montenegro decided to stay in a federation with Serbia. Spengler writes, "When we say an event is epoch-making, we mean that it marks in the course of a culture a necessary and fateful turning point" ([1926] 1961:148). The Bolshevik Revolution of 1917 was epoch making in this sense, because it achieved the "idea" of the French Revolution, the transition from culture to civilization. Ever since 1917, Soviet society had been trying to achieve the Western miracle based on science, industry, and the "systematic spirit," and such an undertaking, in Spengler's view, is narrow, "autumnal," and fated to die (p. 152). One might wonder whether the final collapse of Soviet Communism in 1991 was an epoch-making event or just an episode in the process that began with the Bolshevik Revolution. This is an important question to which an analysis based on Spengler leads. Again, our aim in this book is to explore some possible answers and to expose the importance of this and related questions, not to arrive at a definitive answer.

Spengler was a pessimist because he did not believe that history could reverse itself. The process of civilization, once set into motion, cannot revert back to culture. Thus, if one takes Spengler seriously, one would predict that there exist only two realistic scenarios for the future of post-Communist lands in Eastern Europe and the former Soviet Union. Either the civilizational ideas that gave rise to Communism in the first place will reassert themselves in a new, autocratic, expansionist form, or Western capitalism—which is itself an expansionist product of late civilization—will take the place of Communism but will lead not to the desired peace and social order but to new instability and chaos.

Even if one chooses to reject Spengler's pessimistic appraisal of history, it is important to realize what is at stake in this discussion. Leading critiques of American decadence by Bell (1976), Bellah et al. (1985), Bloom (1987), Lasch (1991), and others conclude by positing the need for a magical return to some by-gone era of republicanism, community, sharing, and other "good" aspects of American history and culture. Spengler's analysis posits, by contrast, that history cannot be reversed and that these "good" aspects of early America will never be recovered. In fact, he argues that such nostalgia is itself a symptom of late civilization, which "looks back piteously to its childhood, then finally, weary, reluctant, cold, it loses its desire to be, and, as in Imperial Rome, wishes itself out of the overlong daylight and back in the darkness of protomysticism, in the womb of the mother, in the grave" (p. 104). The postmodernist movement has institutionalized such nostalgia and protomysticism in the New Age books, the revival of fundamentalism, the love of museum culture, and the constant copying and recycling of early films, novels, and songs (see Meštrović 1991 and Rosenau 1992).

If Bellah et al. (1985) and other critics of late American culture are correct that the postmodernist movement promotes cancerous individualism at the expense of integrative forces, one should wonder why Americans in particular and Westerners in general would want to impose such a troubling aspect of American/Western culture onto post-Communist lands. Moreover, from Spengler's perspective, the implicit belief by Bellah and other critics that American habits of the heart can be fixed through proper social engineering not only is erroneous but betrays the systematic spirit that is characteristic of decaying civilizations. Even if Spengler is wrong in his analysis of Western history, it is important to consider him, if for no other reason than to maintain some sort of objectivity in discussions of this sort, which tend to be ideological and wildly optimistic.

Another important consequence of Spengler's analysis is that it helps to explain how and why Communism took root in Eastern Europe and the former Soviet Union and why it died there as well. The expansionist, imperialist dimension of Communism included an affinity with the expansionist, imperialist social character that was already present in these lands, which Tomašić (1953) traces back to Genghis Khan. Spengler explains that Napoleon represented the forces of late civilization as they defeated medieval culture, even though he himself was defeated by civilizational forces at Waterloo.

It is the idea that counts, not its outward form for Spengler and other German, fin-de-siècle thinkers like him (most notably, Georg Simmel, who also makes much of the distinction between life and its forms). Similarly, it could well be the case that Communism is itself a product of late civilization, and even if capitalism seems to have defeated Communism and "won" the Cold War, the idea of late civilization persists in all its decadent and decaying manifestations. In such a pessimistic reading of Western history, neither side won the Cold War. Western culture lost the battle with civilization long ago, at least according to Spengler.

Culture and Cross-national Perceptions: Germany Continued

It is worth reminding the reader that our purpose here is not to understand German culture per se but to lay the theoretical groundwork and context for the analysis of Slavic culture. Nevertheless, an interesting test of Veblen's and Spengler's views with regard to imperial Germany's cultural lag and uneven transition into late civilization is to take into account the changes in contemporary Germany. Is contemporary Germany perceived by neighboring countries as less of a threat than it used to be? Overall, the reply seems to be affirmative. France and England no longer fear that Germany will attack them for the sake of territory.

But vestiges of the old habits and reactions to those habits remain. England's former prime minister Margaret Thatcher was fond of referring to Germany as the Hun. When Germany declared that it wanted to support Croatian and Slovene independence—two nations that used to be part of the old Austro-Hungarian Empire—England and France accused Germany of wanting to revive a nostalgia for empire building. Subsequently, England and France blocked European Community efforts, led by Germany, to come to the aid of Croatia. As late as March of 1992, England and France protested the cost of sending peacekeeping troops to the war-torn

Balkans, and their protests hindered the deployment of these troops. Can anyone doubt that old habits really do persist much more powerfully than modernists like to admit? There exist other ambiguities. Extremist groups in post-Communist, unified Germany do claim that Austria as well as portions of Poland, former Czechoslovakia, and Slovenia are really German. Skinheads and neo-Nazi groups captured headlines in the 1990s with their racist and anti-immigrant actions and statements. Beyond a doubt, these are fringe elements within German society, but they testify to the fact that it would be a mistake to apply the end-of-history or other modernist thesis to Germany or any other modern society today.

Finally, it should be noted that even if Germany is no longer perceived to be a military threat in the contemporary world, it—along with Japan—is definitely perceived to be an economic threat. According to Veblen, Spengler, Sorokin, and other pessimists from the previous turn of the century, economic imperialism lays the groundwork for and can be converted easily into old-fashioned military imperialism. Could it be that the archaic, bellicose habits of the fight that interested Veblen have been muted into economic competition, but have not disappeared completely? Such a conclusion would be entirely in keeping with Veblen's and Spengler's cultural analyses.

German culture is an important topic for the present analysis not only because it serves as a vehicle for discussing the linkage between Veblen's and Spengler's analyses of German imperialism with Tomašić's analysis of the cultural groundwork for Slavic totalitarianism. In addition, Germany broke ranks with the European Community to recognize Croatia in 1991, and in general, Germany disagreed frequently with NATO countries and especially the United States regarding policies toward the Soviet Union in the 1970s and 1980s. Stephen Kalberg (1987, 1989, 1991) has written extensively on the link between German political culture and cross-national perceptions in a manner that is commensurate with the cultural analyses we have thus far reviewed. We turn our attention next to

Kalberg's analyses of contemporary Germany in order to elaborate further on the fundamental sociological assumption in the present work, namely, that far from being objective or universal, political perceptions and decisions are shaped by the distinct culture or habits of thought in a nation, and these are derived from previous habits of the heart.[2]

Kalberg (1991:36) reviews the fact that "in the United States, political freedoms and personal liberties have always been understood as involving freedom from state interference." Bellah et al. (1985) and other analysts of American habits of the heart would certainly concur. This is probably one reason among many why the Americans consistently viewed the strong state of the former USSR with fear and anger, and why many American analysts felt that capitalism and democracy would have a chance in the former USSR only if Moscow lost its central power.

But the Germans have always had a strong state tradition, Kalberg argues, and he underscores a similar insight by Veblen. According to Kalberg (1991:37), "Since Bismarck, the state has been perceived as properly assisting and guiding industrialization, as responsible for employment and economic stability, and as a protector of the public's welfare against a capitalist economic system widely perceived as flawed and exploitative." In contrast to American traditions that drew on the Enlightenment and classical liberalism, nineteenth-century Germans embraced Romanticism, which in turn abhorred the isolated individual and praised the communal aspects of the gemeinschaft. An excellent illustration of this Romantic trend as it was expressed sociologically is Ferdinand Tönnies's 1887 sociological classic *Community and Society (Gemeinschaft und Gesellschaft)*. If Bellah et al. (1991) are correct to extrapolate from Tocqueville that Americans need to temper their individualism, lest it become cancerous, and need to nurture a community spirit, it would seem that the opposite is true for German culture.

Thus, in the United States, national heroes tend to be political figures, and American civil religion tends to be militant; consider portrayals of Washington, Jefferson, Lincoln, Roosevelt, and

Kennedy and the monuments, holidays, and symbols associated with them. By contrast, ideal figures in Germany are philosophers, writers, and scholars, such as Kant, Goethe, Schiller, Hegel, Schopenhauer, and Nietzsche. What is the connection between holding philosophers as cultural heroes and the emphasis on a strong state, Romanticism, and perhaps even barbarism? Veblen ([1915] 1964:108) explains:

> German speculation and inquiry took what has been called a profounder character, in that attention turned habitually to ulterior and transcendental systematisations of the knowledge in hand and to a quest of realities in the domain of the spirit, that is to say, in rationalized terms of personal force and spiritual congruity; *the rationalization taking its color from the regime of mastery and submission, orderly subservience to an authentically imposed scheme of conventional values.* The culmination, of course, is German metaphysics of the Romantic school, *drawn on lines of logical congruence rather than of efficient causation, and reaching its ultimate in the quasi-pantheistic over-ruling dominance of a transcendental personality.* . . . This work of the human spirit as it has come into play under the German habituation is spoken of as "nobler," "profounder," —a point not to be disputed [emphasis added].

It is fascinating that, by contrast, Tocqueville felt that there had never been and never would be a genuinely great American writer. He explained this conviction by noting that, at bottom, almost everyone in America feels equal to everyone else, so that even great talent is less respected in America than it would be in Germany or elsewhere in the world. For a contemporary illustration of this cultural difference, consider that even as late as 1992, university professors in Germany are addressed with three titles denoting respect, literally, "Mr. Professor Dr. _____." An American professor is lucky to receive even one respectful appellation.

The important point is that, combining insights from Veblen and Kalberg, we note that a culture that tends toward barbarism and autocratic control over the individual has tended historically to produce nobler, deeper, and more profound philosophy than cultures that tend toward individualism, human rights, and utilitarianism.

It would be interesting, indeed, to explore further whether habits of the heart that press toward practicality and equality diminish what used to be called cultural richness. Russian and other Slavic cultures may be classified as being closer to the German model being elaborated here than is American, English, or French culture. Can one imagine an American equivalent to Tolstoi, Dostoevsky, or Goethe? We are touching here on the controversial thesis that cultural pessimism may be related to a less democratic but also a more profound culture, in comparison with democratic but bland cultures (see Bailey 1958; Kalberg 1987; Meštrović 1991; Tocqueville 1845).

Another point of comparison and contrast taken up by Kalberg is Tocqueville's finding that Americans are irritatingly patriotic, whereas "German national identity remains a broken one" (Kalberg 1991:39). Kalberg adds that "a normal sense of nationalism is still in the process of developing, as is a strong self-identification as German." Kalberg does not delve into the issue whether Germans possessed a "normal" sense of nationalism in 1915, the year in which Veblen wrote his book on imperial Germany and warned against its bellicose patriotism. One wonders how the rise of Nazism can be explained if Germans are not nationalistic. Perhaps Kalberg is implying that American civil religion is much more organized and self-consciously promoted in the United States than is German civil religion. For example, in America one commonly encounters frequent displays of the flag, the singing of the national anthem before sports events, the recitation of the pledge of allegiance in school, and similar events. While Robert Bellah (1967) has explored manifestation of American civil religion, there does not exist a comparable analysis of its German counterpart.

Nevertheless, we have arrived at an important issue: if German sense of nationhood remains broken, one could argue that following Communism, scores of national self-identities that were taken for granted suddenly seemed problematic. Yugoslav self-identity became splintered, along with Soviet, Czechoslovak, and other similar collective identities. The responses to this splintering varied tremendously. Following the dissolution of Yugoslavia, the Slovenes seem to have developed the least bellicose national civil religion and were apparently content to enjoy their own, limited, nonexpansive national identity. By contrast, Serbia responded by trying to restore a Greater Serbia, while Croatian civil religion seems to have taken a middle path: more ostentatious than the Slovenes, it never reached the imperialist pitch exhibited by the Serbs.

Kalberg points out that the American, Puritan heritage was established on the premise of world mastery, which constituted a sharp departure from previously held, classical notions of ethical life. Harking back to Spengler's terminology, one might characterize American civil religion as having been established more on the basis of expansionist civilization as opposed to self-contained culture. By contrast, Kalberg claims that German Lutheranism and Catholicism failed to develop asceticism bent upon world mastery. Kalberg's analysis is commensurate with Max Weber's (1904) own criticisms of German Lutheranism as being insufficient to produce the expansionist social character necessary for capitalism. All this may be true, but Kalberg fails to explain the origins of German expansionism that led to the two world wars. As we have seen, Veblen attributes this aspect of German social character to an unhappy persistence of barbarism, whereas Spengler attributes it to the forces of civilization.

For the purposes of our discussion, the important point that emerges is that every nation displays conflicting cultural tendencies, some tending in outward, expansionist directions, while others are inner and promote self-contentment. Thus, American Protestantism tended in an expansionist direction, while the small town meeting that fascinated Tocqueville may be regarded as America's cultural aspect. Kalberg's analysis is useful in pointing out that compared with the Americans, German social character never embraced capitalism or "rugged individualism" and therefore expressed more sympathy toward socialism than Americans have.

Kalberg points out that America may be regarded as a competitive culture in which a strong political left is absent: progress is assumed to be an integral aspect of American civil religion. By contrast, "among nineteenth-century industrializing nations, anti-modernity, anti-capitalism and cultural pessimism [*Kulturpessimismus*] appear to have been most widespread in Germany" (p. 45). After all, Germany produced a Schopenhauer and Nietzsche, while America could not. But this cultural difference led to several important political differences between Germans and Americans. The Germans sought a paternal social welfare state to protect them from the shocks and disruptions of industrialization, whereas Americans were always suspicious and contemptuous of the welfare state, even during the Great Depression. "The United States has unequivocally embraced modern technology," whereas in Germany "a strong streak of ambivalence toward modern technology has been apparent over the last 100 years" (p. 46). Whereas Americans were eager to promote gesellschaft (society), the Germans perceived the "potential of modern technology to destroy the *Gemeinschaft* (community) and to leave individuals adrift and without firm social ties" (p. 46).

Perhaps one of the most important consequences of these differences in cultural perceptions between Germany and the United States is that the Germans consistently regarded the Soviets as technologically backward, whereas "the Americans, on the other hand, never cultivated such negative stereotypes of the Russian people or of Soviet technology. Instead, they have consistently taken Soviet technological advances quite seriously, indeed, so much so, that Soviet technological prowess has been frequently overestimated" (p. 47). This last point requires elaboration. It seems to be the case that well up to the last days of the Cold War, the CIA grossly overestimated Soviet technology and therefore the Soviet threat. As a result, the fall of the Soviet empire took the CIA and the U.S. government in general by surprise. This emerged as an important point of contention during the confirmation hearings of Robert Gates as the new director of the CIA.

The important point seems to be that the United States overestimated its opponent in the Cold War because of its own proclivity toward technological expansion: it was a case of projecting American national perception onto the world. The Germans, in contrast, were consistently less enamored with modernity and its fruits, including capitalism, the doctrine of unending progress, and optimism. This factor led them to perceive the Soviet threat, or lack of it, in more realistic terms. In addition, it points to affinities with Veblen's and Spengler's analyses, both of whom regarded modernity and expansionism as latecomers onto the German cultural scene.

Implications

Zbigniew Brzezinski (1989) is undoubtedly correct that Communism took over at the turn of the previous century under the faith that the new century would be a century of reason rather than one of passion. Such an attitude toward human rationality at the expense of passion is typical of modernity after the turn of the century (Bauman 1991; Meštrović 1991) and is shared by the capitalist West. In any event, it is true that the Soviet and other Communists did all they could to repress and deny all aspects of what they termed Western, bourgeois *irrationalism*. Brzezinski (1989:47) quotes Yevgeniy Afanasyev on Radio Budapest on November 7, 1987, as making the following comment about Soviet Communism in this century: "We did not concern ourselves with Max Weber or Durkheim, or Freud, or Toynbee, or Spengler. These are not just names, they are names which have worlds, world systems behind them. If a society fails to acquaint itself with these worlds, it simply falls out of the twentieth century, it finds itself on the periphery of the most important discoveries of the century."

Indeed, Marxism and Communism regarded the thinkers listed above as decadent, bourgeois pessimists (Lukàcs 1980). Note the ironic fact that from the *cultural* perspective taken by these and other fin-de-siècle thinkers who were repressed, Marxism and Communism were destined to fail because they constitute arrogant attempts at social engineering. From Max Weber's ([1904] 1958) perspective, twentieth-century Communism had to trap its citizens into an "iron cage" because it ignored the spirit of its people. Durkheim

(1928) predicted the eventual demise of socialism as well as Communism—even as these were just being formed in his time—because both were erected on the premise that human egoism and the lower pole of *homo duplex* in general could be overcome through social engineering. Freud never believed in utopias of any sort and consistently wrote about Marxism with a mixture of incredulity and contempt. Toynbee and Spengler felt that Communism's abstractionism, expansionism, and imperialism were symptoms of the last stage of civilization as we know it in the West. Spengler in particular wrote extensively about a civilization's inescapable *destiny*, despite its optimistic faith that any problem could be solved through methods borrowed from the natural sciences. Communism was doomed to fail from the start, but this is because its starting point was a hardened, calcified socialist doctrine bent on the will to power—a doctrine possible only in the last stages of civilization.

In this chapter, as well as the book as a whole, we have taken seriously Spengler, Toynbee, Weber, Durkheim, Freud, Veblen, Sorokin, Tocqueville, Tomašić, and other cultural theorists whose thought deserves to be labeled as pessimistic (Bailey 1958). But not only the Communists have disregarded these thinkers—they have been neglected relative to the defenders of modernism in capitalist Western lands as well. In this regard, both sides of what used to be the Cold War may have fallen out of the twentieth century, in Afanasyev's words. Communism indeed fell first, but that is not a good reason to think that capitalism—at least in its present form, as a trajectory of Adam Smith's thought and the late civilization that served as its context—will not also fall.

For example, in *The True and Only Heaven*, Christopher Lasch (1991) links the expansionist doctrine of capitalism to Adam Smith's recognition several centuries ago that human passions are infinite. This infinity of passions (deemed anomic by Durkheim) was supposed to fuel unending progress forever. Lasch is correct that this dream cannot come true if for no other reason than that the world will eventually run out of the raw materials that capitalism and industrialization require. From Spengler's perspective, Communism is a product of late civilization every bit as much as capitalism is. The perspectives we have used in this book lead to conclusions that are quite different from those of most foreign affairs experts, analysts, and the media. For example, Zbigniew Brzezinski (1989) spoke for an entire generation when he declared that Communism died in the late 1980s in Eastern Europe and the former Soviet Union because of American efforts in the Cold War and because of Soviet economic incompetence. Spengler and other cultural analysts would offer a different interpretation of the same set of facts: Communism fell of its own accord because that was its destiny. But Communism's nemesis was not the capitalist West. Rather, it was the "good" non-Dinaric and non-Ural culture found in Slavic lands. This is a feminine culture, described aptly by Henry Adams as derived from the power of the Virgin, not from the dynamo. However, this feminine culture began to slide into oblivion with the Protestant Reformation in the West and will probably not survive the civilizational forces now poised against it.

Thus, in our reading, Communism is simply one form among many such forms of late civilization's abstract expansionism and lack of culture. This means, along the lines of Tomašić's (1948b, 1953) analyses, that it is very likely that a new form of totalitarianism will emerge out of the ashes of Communism in the lands that it used to rule. Along the lines that were crystallized in Horkheimer and Adorno's *Dialectic of the Enlightenment*, Western, so-called democratic nations are also in danger of losing sight of the original habits of the heart that gave rise to liberal ideals several centuries ago.

We can expose more clearly in what ways our interpretation of the collapse of Communism differs by comparing our conclusions with those reached by Brzezinski in his book *The Grand Failure: The Birth and Death of Communism in the Twentieth Century* (1989). To begin with, we disagree with the implications in the title. Communism was not born in the twentieth century but developed out of expansionist forms of civilization that Spengler traces to Napoleon and the birth of Protestantism. And we do not believe that Communism died. In the first place, it still rules China and a good portion of the population of Asia, not to mention Serbia, Monte-negro, and Albania, among others. In fact, as of 1992, more people lived under Communist forms of government than lived under de-mocracy. But this is a technicality, albeit an important one. Com-munism did not die because its "idea" has not been extinguished. This idea is rooted in civilizational expansionism, which manifested itself in the Serbian grab for territory in the Yugoslav War that be-gan in 1991 and will probably manifest itself in Russian imperial-ism at the expense of its member states in the new commonwealth founded by Boris Yeltsin.

We agree with Brzezinski (1989:8) that Communist societal "reconstruction was to be achieved through the direct use of state power, crushing traditional social forms and eliminating any mani-festations of social spontaneity." But, we would ask, how is this abstract will to power displayed by the Communists different from that appearing in the European Community or in the American ex-pansion of the state at the expense of traditional habits of the heart? America has come a long way from Tocqueville's descriptions of the small town meeting, the intense religiousness of those small towns, and the aristocracy of the legal profession—conservative fac-tors that he felt would offset a dangerous progression into individ-ualism and excessive state power. In the present fin de siècle, the state in the United States and Western Europe seems to perform most of the social functions that used to fall to family, church, and neighborhood.

According to Brzezinski, the Communist idea of the state was that it would cope with economic and social ills, an idea that turned out to be fallacious. It is a model of social welfare based on human rationality alone, at the expense of the heart, and proved to be wasteful and ineffectual. Bureaucracy, abstractionism, and the im-personality of the state simply cannot substitute for the old-fashioned, emotional, integrative habits of the heart. Brzezinski points out that the Third World looked to the Soviet model as the best and fastest road to modernity and social justice, and he is clearly critical of that model (p. 9). But again, we would point out that this model is not fundamentally different *in practice* from the Western model. The Western welfare states are also extremely wasteful, inefficient, and cumbersome, although perhaps they have not yet reached the level of Soviet inefficiency. But given all the economic scandals of the past few decades in the West—especially the widespread fear in America that the entire banking and Social Security systems are on the brink of financial disaster—it is not evident that the Western system is truly superior. Our point is that both protagonists in the Cold War exhibit similar assumptions about the exclusive role of an expansionist state and human rationality.

The Soviets, however, never produced a single consumer good that could compete on the world market. The Yugo automobile—that product of the "cutting edge of Serbo-Croatian technology," as it was mocked in the film *Dragnet*—was a complete failure in the United States. But Brzezinski never considers the problem that worries Lasch (1991) and other critics of consumer-based progress: Once the post-Communists become like the West and develop a consumer-based economy, they will inherit all of the problems that go along with such an economy, including anomie.

We agree with Brzezinski that Gorbachev based his legitimacy on Leninism because he had to: the only other indigenous choices would have come from pre-Bolshevik history, which is anything but democratic. In this sense, Gorbachev was destined to fail in his quest for perestroika because the outward form of reformed Leninism that he represented was itself doomed. But what cultural forces does his successor, Boris Yeltsin, represent? Yeltsin speaks the language of free-market forces and democratic institutions, yet our analysis would raise two somewhat cynical reservations about his intentions: (1) This language, which is amenable to the West, may mask the resurgence of pre-Bolshevik, autocratic cultural habits, and (2) one may question whether a genuine free-market or representative democracy as it was practiced in Tocqueville's days exists any longer. The West may be trying to sell to the formerly Communist nations a cultural product under false advertising.

5. Explaining War in the Land of Medjugorje

Max Weber's ([1904] 1958) fame rests in large measure on his analyzing an obvious affinity between Protestantism and capitalism (cf. Käsler 1988). In this book, we are interested in a parallel to that famous affinity, namely, the connection between Catholic and Orthodox religions and Communism, as well as the role of these religions in the post-Communist reconstruction. How did Communism take root in cultures that are not only non-Protestant but, in many ways, pre-Protestant? How can one explain the brutality of the Yugoslav War that began in 1991 in the land of Medjugorje, the site of the Virgin Mary's "appearances" since 1981? (From here on, we shall drop the quotations from the word "appearances," but always with the understanding that we are invstigating the sociological, not the theological, implications of these appearances.) These are vast, neglected questions, and we shall attempt to do no more than sketch a basis for meaningful replies in the pages that follow.

Another one of our aims is to follow up on a prediction made by Meštrović in the Coming Fin de Siècle that Medjugorje is the Fatima of our times and symbolizes "the yearning of Slovenia and Croatia in the West for greater pluralism and democracy versus the Serbian leanings in the East for fascist-like nationalism and monolithic political systems" (1991:152). As such, it is not a coincidence that Medjugorje, which is situated in Bosnia-Hercegovina near the Croatian border, is also situated on a cultural border between these two opposing political tendencies.

Prior to Max Weber's *Protestant Ethic and the Spirit of Capitalism* (1904), Emile Durkheim, in 1893, was among the first social scientists to regard religion primarily as a manifestation of culture, as a symbolic expression of a particular society's conscious as well as unconscious aspirations, values, and total makeup. Society is the patient, the sociologist is the analyst, and religious myths and symbols are the symptoms in this scheme of things. Spengler (1926) and other cultural analysts from the previous fin de siècle also approach religion in this manner. When one examines the particulars of the religious culture in Eastern Europe and the Soviet Union from this cultural perspective, one finds, in addition to the theodicy of suffering, far more emphasis on the cult of Mary than on the cult of Jesus. This is bound to be a significant factor in explaining the orientation of the underlying culture that survived Communism. It also exposes a neglected but obvious aspect of Max Weber's famous analysis of Protestantism, namely, that it is primarily a Jesus-oriented religion.

Max Weber treats Catholicism in a purely negative light, as a traditional body of cultural thought that prevents, delays, or otherwise gets in the way of the rise of capitalism. It seems never to have occurred to Weber that Catholicism has a *positive* function, that it preserves the culture, community, and nonutilitarian individualism that is of interest to Spengler, Tomašić, Tönnies, Toynbee, and other cultural analysts. In this way, too, Weber displays a Hegelian bent. Hegel (1899) had argued that German Protestants, in particular, would achieve the desired, rational state of the end of history. For the purposes of our analysis, we wonder how and why Communism could have taken hold of these cultures. Several hypotheses are possible, on the basis of the preceding analysis. Catholic and Orthodox emphases on the "heart," or compassion, as opposed to the emphasis on the "mind" characteristic of expansionist civilizations (according to Spengler) held out some affinity with Communist and socialist ideals of humanism and egalitarianism. But these humanitarian ideals were infused by the Communists with a tendency toward a will to power not present in pre-Protestant religions.

In this regard, we agree with Spengler ([1926] 1961:361) that "in spite of its foreground appearances, ethical Socialism is *not* a system of compassion, humanity, peace and kindly care, but one of will-to-power." One might thus hypothesize that this systematic, power-hungry version of socialism would be a prime candidate for displacing the humanitarian ethics characteristic of Orthodox and Catholic religions. Much research will be necessary before this issue can be resolved.

We caution against treating Protestant, Catholic, or Orthodox expressions of Jesus or Mary in a universal, positivistic manner. The meaning of these symbols varies from culture to culture and from epoch to epoch, so that all continuities are relative. Erich Fromm (1963) has already demonstrated that the collective meaning of Jesus varies tremendously across the centuries; something similar should follow for the representations associated with female goddesses, including the Virgin Mary.[1] For example, instead of the symbol of Christ transforming modernity, modernity has transformed Christ from the *feminine* Christ who loved children and was symbolized by the Good Shepherd to the tough, militant Christ who battles Satan for supremacy of the world. The modern version of Christ is entirely commensurate with the expansionist, will-to-power dimensions cited by Spengler (1926) and many other cultural analysts. To the best of our knowledge, no study has traced systematically and scientifically the cultural meanings and sociological implications of the representations of Mary since the fourth century up to Medjugorje.

Along these cultural dimensions, in "The Dynamo and the Virgin," the American novelist and cultural analyst Henry Adams ([1901] 1983) uses the Great Exposition of 1900 to suggest that modernity is symbolized by the power of the dynamo, whereas medieval European culture derived its power from the Virgin. He points to representations of the Virgin at Chartres, Notre Dame, the Louvre, and other well-known landmarks to conclude that the Virgin was the highest energy ever known to humankind, the creator of four-fifths of the noblest art, exercising vastly more attraction over the human mind than all the steam engines and dynamos ever dreamed of. And yet, according to Adams, this energy was unknown to the American mind. An American Virgin would never dare command; an American Venus would never dare exist.

All this may have some truth to it. For the purposes of our analysis, however, one would like to know how the representations of the Virgin at Chartres compare with the representations of the Virgin at Medjugorje. Above all, how has the "power" derived from the Virgin come to take on a militant tone in the Balkans? We do not pretend to have found the answers to these questions but insist only that they are important questions that need to be addressed in the near future.

In any event, Eastern European culture is still dominated more by the symbol of the Virgin than by that of the dynamo, and the reverse is true in Western Europe and the United States. Erich Fromm's (1963) analyses of mother-centered cultures from Mexico to medieval Europe as fostering a passive character orientation still seem applicable to Eastern Europe. Fromm argues that the cultural worship of the Madonna and Child Jesus leads to identification with the helpless child, Jesus. In sharp opposition to the emphasis on self-help found in Puritan and subsequent Protestant civilizations— erected on the motto that God helps those who help themselves (Mumford 1955)—mother-centered cultures should be more amenable to various forms of welfare programs and state control. Even in their personal lives, the former Yugoslavs still typically regard their mothers as confidants and as being more important than their spouses. Shrines to the Madonna abound throughout the Balkans, in Catholic as well as Orthodox cultures.

Tomašić on the Connection between Mother-centered Culture and Communism

Tomašić (1953:95) observes that in Slavic lands, the mother's role becomes one of intercessor and protector against the wrath of the father. Is it not interesting that the Virgin Mary, mother of Jesus, is depicted in precisely this way in relation to the wrathful God the Father? The Christian symbolism of Eastern Europe reflects the family patterns uncovered by Tomašić as much as the Christian symbolism in Western Europe and the United States reflects the essential egalitarianism discovered by Tocqueville. In the Protestant West, Jesus is a far more important figure than the Virgin Mary, or any other carryover from female goddesses of the past. By contrast, the former USSR and Eastern Europe are predominantly Orthodox or Catholic, and both of these religions focus on the Virgin Mary. In fact, these faiths worship Mary more than God the Father or Jesus or the Holy Spirit—she is the center of idolatry, art, theology, and folk worship (cf. Petro 1990).

In a Durkheimian context, the dominance of masculine representations of deity marks the dominance of values appropriate to modern and postmodern societies based on the dynamo, namely, rationality, self-control, duty, and the other virtues described by Max Weber. The more ancient and basic female goddesses represented compassion, fertility, humility, the oneness and totality of the universe, and a premodern orientation in which the world was comprehended as a womb. Max Weber does not give much attention to the fact that Catholic symbolism, which he dismissed as traditional and therefore unsuited to capitalism, provides for the survival of ancient goddess worship in a culture in which mother- and female-oriented values are functional.

For example, Tomašić (1953:107) writes that as a result of the Dinaric father's rejection and harsh nature, "identification with a humiliated and suffering mother might foster or reinforce sympathy" in general and with the suffering masses, not to mention suffering Russia. He continues that "in Russia feelings of rejection and identification with those who suffer gave a strong emotional support to ideologies which sought a messianic salvation of all suffering humanity," especially the common people. In addition, "We find the urge for destruction and identification with suffering as fundamental aspects of the ideology of Russian revolutionary movements" (Tomašić 1953:109).

Not only Communism but great Slavic literature from the nineteenth and early twentieth centuries expressed a preoccupation with social, political, and religious problems of humankind. Compassion for the weak and suffering was extolled as the primary virtue. As illustration, simply compare the Western focus on morality derived from cold-hearted, rational duty, found in writers from Kant to Kohlberg, with Tolstoi's and Dostoevsky's moving sermons on compassion. According to Tomašić (1953:114):

> Sympathy for those who suffer and identification with them is an outstanding trait of Russian literature of the nineteenth and early twentieth centuries. Russian writings of those days exhibit a preoccupation with great social, political, religious, and psychological problems of mankind. They picture a gloomy, painful, and tragic world, full of misery, injustice, blood and death. In the same manner the school textbooks of those days contained many heartbreaking stories full of compassion and commiseration for the suffering, unprotected weak.

Spengler ([1925] 1961:361) makes much of the fact that in the West, "the head and front of moral modernity must ever be Kant, who excludes from his ethics the motive of compassion." One might also note that except for Schopenhauer's (1841) polemic with Kant on the issue of compassion's role in morality, most Western moralists, professors, and civilization as a whole followed Kant in rejecting compassion as the basis for morality.[2] Thus, we have uncovered a tremendous contrast between the West and East that follows in the wake of the distinction between Jesus and Mary, rationality and compassion, respectively. But again, what concerns us here more than anything else is why and how the compassionate cultures that preceded Communism gave rise to tremendous bloodshed and violence.

There exists a real danger that violence might follow the second Russian Revolution, of 1991, just as it did after the Bolshevik

Revolution of 1917. Following the demise of Communism, contemporary Eastern Europeans and citizens of the former USSR are still seeking a more humane alternative to what they consider to be ruthless capitalism. Despite Boris Yeltsin's and other former Communist leaders' embrace of free-market economics through "shock therapy," there is no good reason to suppose that the cultural basis of formerly Communist lands has been transformed from compassion and identification with a suffering humanity to Protestant-based self-interest. According to Tomašić (1953:115), Russian social character is profoundly ambivalent with regard to these traits:

> Fear and awe, submission and sense of guilt are rooted in the structure of the Great Russian society and are supported by its traditions. But so is compassion, humility, demand for truth and justice and for egalitarian acceptance, as well as revolt and terror, lack of trust and urge to destroy. It is the propensity to experience such contrasting sentiments that causes behavior which is alternatively bent in opposite directions.

Thus, Tomašić complements Fromm's (1955) analysis of mother-centered passivity and submission by noting that Slavic cultures inculcate *both* self-reliance modeled after the tough father *and* submission modeled after the submissive, all-forgiving mother: "The attraction to an unapproachable and unattainable father and the feeling of revolt against his despotism, seeking solace from mother and reaction against her over-protection might cause a constant alternation between extremes of these emotional reactions [self-reliance versus submission]" (Tomašić 1953:98).

In addition, according to Tomašić (1953:106) if Slavic cultures worship motherhood, they likewise denigrate the old woman: "The folk image of the woman is in remarkable contrast to the image of the mother. The derisive name for woman is *baba*, and baba is said not to be a human being, according to a proverb, therefore mistreatment and abuse of women may be justified." Tomašić's observation still rings true in 1991 Eastern Europe and the former Soviet Union, compared with American and Western European civilizations, which stress the equality of males and females in accordance with liberal doctrine.

In these regards, the apparitions of the Virgin Mary since 1981 in Medjugorje,[3] Bosnia-Hercegovina, are an interesting link to her many alleged apparitions in the last century, when she also symbolized resistance to a victorious modernity in general and capitalism in particular (see Meštrović 1991:136–62). Is this still her cultural significance at Medjugorje, with the caveat that Communism be added to the modernist doctrines that she resists? Since the previous turn of the century, at least in the West, the cult of Jesus has become much more dominant, in keeping with Henry Adams's observations. The cultural values associated with the modernist Jesus seem to be very harsh, if not militant. Jesus used to be the Good Shepherd in artistic depictions at the turn of the century; now he has taken over the role of judge ascribed by Calvin to God the Father. In the West, Jesus is constantly portrayed as battling Satan in a struggle to dominate the world. This is an expansionist representation of Jesus, commensurate with the expansionist characteristic of modernity. It is another instance of Spengler's belief that Christianity did not transform modernity, but modernity transformed Christianity. In fact, postmodern Protestants seem to pray to Jesus more than to God the Father. This shift in meaning seems to signal a significant cultural departure since Max Weber's *Protestant Ethic*, as suggested by Henry Adams.

One would expect major differences in the origins and functions of the ideology of Jesus versus the ideology of Mary. Eastern European nationalism and ethnocentrism indeed often spill over into militancy. But the moral message given by the Madonna, from Medjugorje to Poland, seems to be softer: peace, compromise, pluralism. One has to explain Eastern European and former Soviet machismo, totalitarianism, and terror in the context of a Virgin-based cultural system. Mary seems to represent the other side of the authoritarian, father-dominated Slavic mind-set uncovered by Tomašić (1948b, 1953). The female side represents the "higher," softer, more-civilized aspects of Slavic culture. Thus, we find the messages of Medjugorje coexisting with more violent tendencies to subjugate other peoples, similar to the often-contrasting values represented by mother and father in Slavic culture.

Spengler on Mary's Role in the Decline of the West

We began this chapter with the question, What is the significance of the fact that the Yugoslav war that began in 1991 raged in the country in which the Virgin Mary appeared at Medjugorje? We meant to imply that the question is vital for the rest of Eastern Europe and the former USSR, even if their Marian worship is not as intense as that which surrounds Medjugorje, and even if their so-called ethnic conflict has not yet reached the white heat found in former Yugoslavia. A meaningful reply is extremely difficult to find. On the one hand, the modernists attach no significance whatsoever to the worship of Mary that is found in Roman Catholic and various Orthodox religions. They merely adopt Max Weber's connection between an active, willful Jesus and modern capitalism as if that connection required no further comment, elaboration, or context. On the other hand, there is disagreement on the cultural side. Spengler (1926) focuses on the fact that the rise of the cult of Mary in the fourth century in Western Europe corresponds to the first bud of modernity, the first inklings of civilization as opposed to culture, because Mary symbolizes the phenomenon of *care* for the future and for one's offspring. He would have us believe that classical culture lived in an eternal present, without care for the future or the past. Most of those who are familiar with the writings of Plato, Aristotle, and the other classical Greek philosophers will probably agree with him to some extent. But this living in the present is also precisely the way that Frisby (1986) and many others characterize modernity! Moreover, Spengler does not consider the fact that, at least in the West, the cult of Mary seems to have expired with the onset of Protestantism.[4] (It is as if Spengler and Weber address two halves of a giant puzzle without ever noticing that it needs to be put together. Weber ignores the Marian, Gothic preamble to Calvin, whereas Spengler assumes, with incredible naïveté, that patriarchy simply builds on matriarchy.) If Mary symbolizes modern care, then what does the rise of the militant, Protestant Jesus signify? Does Jesus signify more or less care relative to the cultural meaning of Mary?

We have seen that Henry Adams draws the dividing line between modernity and premodernity somewhat differently. For him, Mary symbolizes the premodern mind-set, and modernity is symbolized by the mechanical dynamo of the late nineteenth century. It makes all the difference in the world which explanation one chooses to follow. In the vulgar modernist version that discounts Mary, a Protestant, Jesus-centered version of modernity can be transplanted easily onto Marian cultures. Followers of this popular paradigm assume that the world is a universal, blank slate upon which Westerners may design the world in their image. By contrast, Spengler's explanation holds that the Marian lands are already on their way toward modernity or civilization but that, despite existing temporally in the twentieth century, they exist mentally and culturally in a time and space that is the Western equivalent of the Dark Ages. And for Henry Adams, the fact that Eastern Europe and the former USSR are still Marian testifies to the fact that these lands still constitute culture, gemeinschaft, or nonmodern phenomena. Since we have already explored Adams, let us delve further into Spengler's relevance for the discussion at hand.

According to Spengler, the analogue to the Gothic, Marian period of Western history is the late period of Egyptian civilization. Thus, Mary and the Child Jesus correspond to Isis and Horus:

> Magian Christianity had elevated Mary as Theotokos, "she who gave birth to God," into a symbol felt quite otherwise than by us. The lulling Mother is as alien to Early-Christian Byzantine art as she is to the Hellenic (though for other reasons) and most certainly Faust's Gretchen, with the deep spell of unconscious motherhood on her, is nearer to the Gothic Madonna than all the Marys of Byz-

antine and Ravennate mosaics. Indeed, . . . the Madonna with the Child answers exactly to the Egyptian Isis with Horus—both are caring, nursing mothers—and that nevertheless this symbol had vanished for a thousand years and more (for the whole duration of the Classical and the Arabian Cultures) before it was reawakened by the Faustian soul. (Spengler [1926] 1961:137).

For Spengler, the nursing Mother represents the beginnings of modernity because she "points into the future, and she is just the figure that is entirely missing in the classical art" (p. 267). By contrast, in classical and Indian art and culture, one finds "a picture of utterly careless submission to the moment and its incidents" (p. 137).

According to Spengler, "The whole panorama of early Gothic mankind is pervaded by something maternal, something caring and patient, and Germanic-Catholic Christianity—when it had ripened into full consciousness of itself and in one impulse settled its sacraments and created its Gothic style—placed not the suffering Redeemer but the suffering Mother in the center of its world picture" (p. 267). Along with Henry Adams, Erich Fromm, and many other commentators on Western culture, Spengler observes that "in the religious art of the West, the representation of Motherhood is the noblest of all tasks" (p. 267). But one should add quickly that Spengler's assessment applies to the *historical,* not the contemporary West, whereas it still applies to many areas of *contemporary* Eastern and Central Europe.

Thus, Croatia is frequently referred to as a Marian nation. It was, along with Slovenia, a part of the Austro-Hungarian Empire and still exhibits, in the 1990s, the "Germanic-Catholic Christianity" that is now part of German, Dutch, and Austrian history. It is as if history did not end in Croatia and Slovenia with the onslaught of Communism but became frozen in time. These two nations constitute a medieval culture that exists in the late twentieth century. To travel to Croatia in 1992 is like stepping into the Gothic past of the West, culturally speaking; the automobiles and other modern artifacts are just a gloss that have not yet displaced the mother-centered culture. We imply nothing derogatory with this analogy. On the contrary, Henry Adams, Spengler, Durkheim, and many other cultural analysts praised the so-called Dark Ages as the noblest period of Western history and cite the Renaissance as the beginning of dissolution and anomie.

But what of Serbia and other Orthodox cultures? Interestingly, Spengler does not equate their worship of Theotokos with the Catholic Mother of God, even if, technically speaking, both symbolize the same Mary. And the Orthodox religions are much more patriarchal than Gothic Roman Catholicism, in which the male priest functions as both mother and father (see Fromm and Maccoby 1970). Spengler regards the Orthodox religions that are derived from Byzantium as Magian cultures and, more specifically, as *civilizations* that are bent on expansion and imperialism and thus already in the late or autumnal phase of their cultural development. In this regard, Serbia and Russia are further along developmentally compared with Croatia and some other regions of Eastern Europe. Again, Spengler would not mean this assessment to be interpreted as a compliment, for he regards "advanced civilizations" as decadent, imperialistic, and dying.

If Spengler might regard the contemporary Orthodox lands as more advanced than the Catholic East and Central Europe, he would not mean this to be interpreted in a positivistic context. He rejects a unilateral, universal view of history. Thus, Russia and Serbia seem to be dominated by a late civilizational phase of Orthodox culture that is advanced only in relation to itself. This view does not imply any absolute superiority or advancement relative to other, neighboring cultures and religions (i.e., Catholic, Protestant, and Muslim). Perhaps the most helpful analogy might be that Serbia and Russia are caught in an expansionist phase of cultural development characteristic of the Protestant Revolution. By contrast, many of their neighbors are existing in a retarded, pre-Reformation, and, one might say, almost medieval cultural mind-set. The religious wars and persecution that characterized Western history as Protestantism broke with traditional Catholicism seem to be repeating themselves, or hold the potential for this Nietzschean recurrence of the same, in the post-Communist lands in which opposing cultural boundaries meet.

Tomašić (1953:201) illustrates some of these connections and affinities that we have been following through Spengler's theoretical perspective: "The Bolsheviks therefore stated that all problems, those of the past and of the present, as well as those of the future, have found their answer in Marxist-Leninist theory. They asserted, however, that this theory is not a dogma. . . . Just as earlier the Russian Orthodox Church had claimed to represent the true Christianity centered in Moscow, the Third Rome, so now the Bolshevik rulers have usurped for themselves the right to represent the true Marxism, centered in the Kremlin."

In sum, using Spengler, one would characterize the cultural situation of the major parties involved in the fall of Communism and its aftermath as follows. First, the West (or the United States and the European Community) is in its last, dying stage of civilization, analogous to Rome shortly before it fell to the barbarians. *The West is autumn.* Second, the westernmost fringes of so-called Eastern Europe (Poland, former Czechoslovakia, Hungary, Croatia, and Slovenia) are in the earliest phases of modern development that is a historical, nostalgic dream to the rest of the West. *They are late spring.* Third, the Orthodox and Muslim cultures that compose the rest of Eastern Europe and portions of what used to be the Soviet Union are in an advanced stage of their own, unique cultural development. *They are late summer.* For the sake of completeness, one could characterize Communism as winter.

For Spengler, from the late summer to the winter of cultural development—more precisely, these cultures are now civilizations— one finds imperialism and expansionism. In early classical, early Western, and the early phases of all cultural developments (including Indian, Egyptian, Chinese, and Arabic), one finds instead of expansionism a passive sticking to one's own frontiers and minding one's own business. Spengler's theory is credible when one considers that at the turn of the previous century, most Western nations, including the United States, were highly imperialistic. The more interesting and neglected aspect of his theory is that Communism is a product of late, Western civilization that wed itself to a Byzantine cultural outlook that was also expansionist and imperialist. Poland, former Czechoslovakia, the Baltics, Hungary, Croatia, Bosnia-Hercegovina and Slovenia were simply caught in the middle of these two expansionist civilizations, each, according to Spengler, in its death throes.

With the fall of Communism, the Western drive for expansionism is more economic than military, at least so far. Capitalism saw the fall of Communism as a marvelous opportunity for expanding its markets. But the late stage of Byzantine or Magian civilization is also bent on expansionism, only it is still the old-fashioned territorial imperialism. In this way, one may explain the Serbian drive to expand its territorial borders following the declarations of independence by Slovenia and Croatia. This might also help to explain Russia's domination of the Commonwealth of Independent States that was created in 1991. In general, if one follows Spengler completely, the Yugoslav case is but an anticipation of what will follow in the former USSR. From the distant West there will come Jesus-centered forces bent on expanding markets and profits. From the Byzantine and Muslim cultures there will also come forces to consolidate and build new empires. The Gothic-Catholic, Marian cultures will be lucky if they can hold their own ground in this colossal aftermath to the Cold War, which is but a prelude to another Cultural War. This is the conclusion to which an analysis based on Spengler leads. In many regards, it is remarkably similar to Tomašić's conclusion that Communism will not die but will merely be transformed into another system based on similar cultural principles.

Medjugorje Reconsidered

As we noted earlier, however, Henry Adams regarded all Marian cultures as fundamentally antimodern. For him, it is the mechanical dynamo, not the care for the future symbolized by the mother, that sets modernity into motion. Let us try to resolve this difficult but important issue by reexamining the Medjugorje phenomenon. We choose it for obvious reasons. Despite the boasting by positivists that religion would have been eliminated by the end of the twentieth century, Medjugorje continues the religious and, more pointedly, Marian tradition that can be traced back to the fourth century in Europe and, after leaping another thousand years, to Isis and Horus. In Spengler's ([1926] 1961:424) words, Medjugorje represents the "second religiousness" that was completely unanticipated by the positivists in their one-sided, imperialistic drive to rule the world by Reason alone:

> Before us there stands a last spiritual crisis that will involve all Europe and America. What its course will be, Late Hellenism tells us. The tyranny of Reason . . . [the] cult of exact sciences, of dialectic, of demonstration, of causality. . . . In this very century, I prophesy, the century of scientific-critical Alexandrianism, of the great harvests, of the final formulations, a new element of inwardness will arise to overthrow the will-to-victory of science. Exact science must presently fall upon its own keen sword. . . . From Skepsis there is a path to "second religiousness," which is the sequel and not the preface of the Culture. Men dispense with proof, desire only to believe and not to dissect. The individual renounces by laying aside books. The culture renounces by ceasing to manifest itself in high scientific intellects.

Spengler helps to explain why Medjugorje has become a postmodern, tourist spectacle for millions of middle-class Westerners, who leave their positivistic worlds and travel to a remote corner of Bosnia-Hercegovina to experience a momentary glimmer of peace. If Medjugorje signifies that Croatia is still Gothic, it signifies also a spectacle of the highest order in a postmodern, dying civilization that seeks nostalgia, faith, and other antidotes to science. In other words, it holds multiple meanings, depending upon which cultural perspective one uses to assess it. What can it mean that the military turmoil that followed the collapse of Communism began in the land of Medjugorje in 1991?

If one begins with the observation that at least since 1830

in Paris, Mary appears only in times of crisis or times that immediately precede a crisis, then her visits to Medjugorje are bound
to be significant. For example, Our Lady of Fatima appeared in 1916,
during the First World War and foreshadowing the ascent of Lenin.
Similarly, Lourdes, Pontmairn, Banneaux, Salette, and the other apparitions corresponded with major social upheavals. In this regard,
Medjugorje was no exception. Mary began her appearances in what
used to be Yugoslavia in 1981, at a time and place that already exhibited more glasnost and perestroika than the Eastern Bloc or the
Soviet Union (one must keep in mind that Communist Yugoslavia
was always closer to the West than the rest of the Communist nations). She kept appearing through the rise and fall of Gorbachev
and his organized, highly publicized versions of glasnost and perestroika, even during the Yugoslav war that began in 1991. Who would
have guessed in the early 1980s that this time around, her apparitions signified what they had signified since the nineteenth century,
namely, that immense social upheavals and crises were just around
the corner? It is easy to suggest that at Medjugorje she fulfilled the
promise at Fatima that Soviet Communism would collapse. But if
Spengler is correct, then her significance for the rest of the modern
world is that she signifies the "second religiousness" that precedes
the collapse of civilization. Is it a coincidence that her appearances
in the present fin de siècle correspond with the rise of the postmodernist discourse?

Moreover, from the cultural perspective we are undertaking
here, it is bound to be highly significant that with Medjugorje, Mary
shifted her appearances from the previous seat of modernity, France,
to a country that served as a harbinger, *again*, of drastic and dramatic
changes in the rest of Eastern Europe and the former USSR. For
example, Croatia and Slovenia were the first to declare their independence from the Communist federation that was Yugoslavia. The
USSR similarly dissolved about six months later. The result of Croatian and Slovenian independence was a hard-line reaction from Serbia and Montenegro, who, remarkably, maintained Communism and
sought to maintain a Yugoslav federation that had always favored

their interests. Only two months after the Serbs attacked Croatia, the hard-liners in Moscow staged a coup against Gorbachev. Perhaps most sadly of all, the bloodshed and hatred on both sides of the Yugoslav conflict and its expansion to neighboring nations (Macedonia, Bosnia, Kosovo) foreshadowed a similar expansion of conflict in the former USSR. In sum, with hindsight, one could claim that the Virgin Mary picked the perfect location for making a symbolic statement.

In general, and in keeping with the import of previous Marian apparitions, the appearances at Medjugorje predated and continue to parallel the social, economic, and political upheaval caused by the collapse of Communism in Eastern Europe and the former USSR. In this sense, Medjugorje will go down in history as another Lourdes and Fatima. But why are major ruptures in the social fabric in the last two centuries of the present millennium presaged by apparitions of the Virgin Mary? Let us construct replies based on the theories of Henry Adams and Oswald Spengler.

Adams would surely point out that compared with the mechanized, dynamic and dynamo-based West, Eastern Europe is still backward. It corresponds to the agricultural, community-based culture that France used to be in the nineteenth century when Mary appeared so many times there. Since Mary's message is steadfastly one of prayer, penance, and faith—classical virtues, completely at odds with utilitarian civilization, to be sure—one might conclude that Mary's apparitions signify the desperate attempts to preserve values based on gemeinschaft prior to the onslaught of gesellschaft. Following Adams, one would predict that once Western capitalism is victorious in Eastern Europe and Medjugorje has its own shopping mall and huge parking lot, the Virgin Mary will stop appearing there or anywhere else in Eastern Europe. She must stop, because she can appear only in the context of a Virgin-centered culture and disappears once the dynamo takes over.

Spengler sees in the Catholic version of the Mother of God the beginnings of a concern with the future and of that active will to power that signals the first stages of modernity, or civilization.

He would have us believe that a classical culture would not have resisted Communism or Western capitalism. It simply would have folded. (In that case, however, one has to wonder what all those wars between Athens and Sparta were about.) If Eastern Europe were like ancient Greece, it would have been completely brainwashed by the Communists, which is what many analysts in America predicted during the Cold War in any event (see Riesman 1954). But the people who were ruled by Communism were *not* brainwashed. The cultures that preceded Communism survived beneath the surface. The fact that Mary appeared in Bosnia-Hercegovina during the height of Communist power in Yugoslavia (power that flowed from the more Byzantine Belgrade, Serbia) symbolizes defiance against the expansionism characteristic of Communist empire building. Medjugorje symbolizes an awakening, a consciousness of national identity that flowered not only in Croatia but across the USSR as Communism collapsed. All those nations that were supposed to have been obliterated by Marxism, which regarded them as false consciousness, instead survived and rose up against the empire.

Medjugorje is located in a remote corner of Bosnia-Hercegovina, a nation-state created in April, 1992, which holds a sizable Muslim minority. Fourteen kilometers from Medjugorje, one encounters the border of Croatia. One could say that the location of Medjugorje symbolizes the dividing line between East and West, the cultures and civilizations that interested Spengler. But then, it has to be significant that the seat of Communism in Yugoslavia was in Serbia, which Toynbee (1978) as well as Spengler regarded as culturally distinct from Western civilization. It cannot be insignificant that Medjugorje is situated on the border of these opposing cultural movements.

Moreover, these two cultural tendencies can be found in all of the Eastern European nations that won their freedom from the former Soviet Union, as well as the nations that used to compose this union. Essentially, it is a conflict between self-determination and the discovery of one's national identity versus a slave-morality that surrenders to the expansionist aims that emanated from Moscow and Belgrade. Following the first apparitions at Medjugorje in 1981 to the present, nationalism has definitely emerged as one of the most powerful cultural forces in formerly Communist nations. The question is, Will nationalism be able to resist not only Moscow and Belgrade but the capitalist expansionist forces from the European Community and the United States? And will it be content to stop at self-determination, or will it spill over into expansionism, the coveting of neighboring nations?

It is important to establish the fact that Medjugorje is not an isolated or unique tribute to the Virgin Mary, as if we were making too much of it. On the contrary, it is typical, as devotions to Mary in Croatia as well as much of the rest of Eastern Europe are *habitual*. In the villages and towns of Croatia on one's approach to Medjugorje, a good many of the Catholic churches are named after Mary. There is the Church of "The Little Lady," The Lady of the Fields," "The Croatian Lady," along with seemingly countless variations on this theme. In some ways, the situation seems analogous to the naming of churches in France during the Renaissance and up to the early part of the nineteenth century. Moreover, these Croatian churches are old, and the cult of the Virgin Mary seems to be hundreds of years old. Old-timers in the region report that before Medjugorje, they knew of many apparitions to many visionaries, and that competing apparitions continue from Poland to Italy through other regions of Croatia. In Spengler's terms, the cultural network concerning the Virgin Mary as Mother of God is old and well established. The cultural construction of the cult of Mary at Medjugorje would not have been possible without this preexisting cultural bedrock.

Still another cultural dimension to the apparitions at Medjugorje can be gleaned from the Serbian reaction. From the very first apparitions in 1981 to the present, the Serbian press coming out of Belgrade has been and continues to be hostile to the Croatian Virgin. The Serbs claim that the Croatian Virgin is appearing at the same geographic location at which thousands of Serbs were killed by pro-Nazi, Croatian Ustaše in World War II. In general, the

Serbian press views the apparitions as disguised Croatian nationalism. This sharp difference in perception among two Christian nations, Croatia and Serbia, regarding a common cult figure, the Mother of God, is inexplicable on purely positivistic grounds. The Croatians and the Serbs, the Catholics and the Orthodox, appear to be too similar on the basis of purely external characteristics to differ so profoundly that they fought against each other on three major occasions in this century (during the two world wars and the civil war of 1991). Our cultural approach explains this divergence on the basis that Croatia and Serbia exist at differing levels of cultural development; specifically, in Spengler's terminology, Serbia is more of an expansionist "civilization" compared with the still-Gothic Croatia. Thus, the Serbian press is correct to cite the political dimensions of the apparitions at Medjugorje, although it omits the fact that Croatia has never shown expansionist tendencies. Over the centuries, its most deeply expressed collective longings have been for independence and autonomy.

Medjugorje and the Theme of Peace

Peace is the cultural phenomenon most associated with Medjugorje. Many devout persons who have made the pilgrimage say that it transformed their lives, that it gave them inner peace. The Vatican has not sanctioned the apparitions, but neither has it condemned them. The Catholic literature on Medjugorje also cites peace as the central, collective message associated with Mary's apparitions. The sermons given at Medjugorje try to alert the world to the need for world peace and for inner, psychic peace. The supreme irony here is that war broke out in Yugoslavia despite Mary's call for peace, and the entire world in the present fin de siècle is far from exhibiting the peaceful new world order that has become a cliché in the United States. What cultural or sociological sense can one make of this?

Spengler is correct to remind scholars that the classical attitude toward any virtue was one of "take it or leave it." An essential component of the ethics taught by both Plato and Aristotle was that virtue must be sought spontaneously for its own sake (a theme mocked by the modernist Nietzsche, who argued that virtue is not its own reward). Spengler points out that even Christ did not try to force his message onto the world but simply invited people to follow him. Similarly, the Medjugorje experience is classical in this sense: the priests present the messages and sermons without that edge of fire and brimstone found in many Protestant sermons in the United States. One is invited to come to Medjugorje to find peace, and if one is not moved, that response seems to be acceptable too. Spengler is also probably correct that modernity tends to change Christianity into a worldview that is more militant and strident and that seeks to fulfill its will to power. In many Protestant sects in the United States especially, one is indoctrinated into joining an army for Christ, one "marches for Jesus," and one is obligated to "witness" publicly for Christ in the hope of gaining converts. The Medjugorje experience lacks these strident dimensions completely.

Medjugorje is thus a relatively unique phenomenon in the modern world in that it offers a classical interpretation of virtue in an otherwise expansionist, imperialist world context. Medjugorje represents the last flicker of classical culture in a civilization that exists in its last stages of development. The situation is somewhat analogous to the cult of Jesus as it tried to gain converts during the last stages of the Roman Empire. We are unable to resolve, however, whether Medjugorje represents the "second religiousness" cited by Spengler, the beginnings of civilization in Eastern Europe, or the beginnings of a new culture that will emerge after the collapse of Communism as well as capitalism in Eastern Europe and what used to be the Soviet Union.

Consider, for example, the difference in the cultural presentation of Medjugorje that would have followed had it occurred in New York or some other modern enclave. It would have been advertised heavily, whereas the Yugoslav government tried to discourage tourists from visiting Medjugorje. It would have been covered by

CNN, whereas Yugoslavia in general seems to be an afterthought for the Western news media. The visionaries would have become celebrities and reaped huge profits off their visions and would have been paraded on all the late-night talk shows. But the further that one follows this thought experiment, the more evident it becomes why Medjugorje could not have occurred in the United States or Western Europe, which, according to Sorokin, Spengler, and Toynbee, are in the last stages of civilizational development. The classical message of peace for its own sake that is offered at Medjugorje could not exist in the context of late civilization, which is bent on the will to power. If late civilization were ever to take up such a cause (i.e., peace), it would not *offer* it in the classical sense but could only *promote* it with all sorts of advertising slogans developed by Madison Avenue. One should add that most such American moral causes invoke war, not peace: consider the wars on AIDS, potholes, litter, poverty, the recession, and many other social ills. Spengler is right to connect Nietzsche's will to power as the essential theme of late civilization.

Why, then, did war break out in Croatia, the land of Mary? First, it should be noted that the Serbs attacked Croatia and sought Croatian territory, not the other way around. Those who hold the classical worldview against the expansionists can be likened to Gandhi, who wrote a famous letter to Hitler asking him to cease his imperialistic and brutal tendencies. Second, as noted by Spengler ([1926] 1961:349), "very feminine natures, too, are capable of brutality—a rebound-brutality of their own—and Greek cruelty was of this kind."[5] (By "feminine," Spengler was referring to the classical philosophy of live and let live and in this sense referred to Hellenic culture as feminine.) If the Serbs exhibited cruelty in the war that began in 1991 for the sake of Greater Serbia and vengeance for past misdeeds against them, the Croatians exhibited cruelty for the idea of an independent Croatia and vengeance for the oppression perpetrated against them.

The entry of Bosnia-Hercegovina in April of 1992 into this latest Balkan War was the decisive event that galvanized Western interest and response. Prior to the siege of Sarajevo, Serbia's aggression against Croatia in 1991 was largely ignored by the West. Moreover, we find it significant that an unexpected outcome of Serbia's attack on Bosnia-Hercegovina was the gradual reemergence of the nonaligned movement and of Islamic self-consciousness. As various Western organizations and nations failed to protect the Muslim minority in Bosnia-Hercegovina from Serbian aggression, various Islamic nations began to organize and to voice the suspicion that the Christian West was engaging in another religious war against Islamic nations. Suddenly, seemingly disparate conflicts in Afghanistan, Somalia, Palestine, Kashmir, Iraq, and Bosnia-Hercegovina were reinterpreted as the East-West conflict that would succeed the Cold War. Only now, the threat would not be Communism, but a perceived Islamic fundamentalism. This, we hold, is the ultimate cultural meaning of Medjugorje in the post-Communist world and the sociological significance of its location in Bosnia-Hercegovina.[6]

6. Conclusions

Our aim in this book has been to offer a cultural explanation as an alternative to the ideologically based explanations of the fall of Communism. If one accepts the ideological explanation that the "evil empire" folded and the West triumphed, then one is not able either to take into account the negative aspects of Western culture or to explain why liberal democracy should take root in the cultural soil that sustained Communism in the first place. Drawing on Alexis de Tocqueville's original and highly regarded *Democracy in America* and its central concept "habits of the heart," we have argued that East and West, America and all the nations emerging from the prison of Communism, must reckon with positive as well as negative aspects of their cultures.

In our explanation, Communism fed on power-hungry values that dominate certain aspects of the many cultures that make up the lands of Eastern Europe and the former USSR. We have argued that the post-Communists will be able to find their own, unique brands of liberal democracy and free-market institutions by relying on their own peaceable cultural traits. Finally, we drew on Veblen, Spengler, and other critics of Western culture to point out that the West is not morally superior in all ways to the former evil empire; it has had, and continues to exhibit, its share of barbaric traits. Our study calls for rapport and genuine, empathetic understanding among the various parties that are involved in the post-Communist drama, not ideological attempts to impose still another round of social engineering on newly freed peoples.

We began this book by observing that the purported end of Communism occurred in the context of a host of other dramatic endings, including the end of the century, millennium, modernity, history, culture, and even sociology (Meštrović 1991). This wider, sociocultural context is crucial for comprehending the end of Communism in our century, for without it, one fails to take into account the postmodernist critiques of the very Enlightenment ideals that are supposed to have triumphed over Communism. But the idea of an ending cannot exist without some indication of a new beginning. Thus, the predominantly apocalyptic conceptual themes of the nineties have been succeeded by conceptualizations of the "new world order," a "new Europe," and the "birth of democracy" in formerly Communist nations. And this vocabulary of new beginnings, in turn, has had to reckon with the return of history (in Fukuyama's sense) and, in general, of old problems that have not gone away, especially nationalism.

The vocabulary of the new apocalypse, which combines the idiom of catastrophic revelations and events ("end," "breakup," "fall," "decline") and utopian idioms ("birth," "triumph," "unity," "new"), has its roots deep in human nature. It must stem from the ambivalent attitude toward death and destruction, as well as the awareness of their inevitability. Moreover, the end of a century or millennium or history or even an entire social system inspires contemporary intellectuals and politicians to believe that their lives and work are unique. This hubris—a particularly human vice, or virtue, depending upon one's point of view—probably has its origins in the human passion for existence and the awareness of the transience of life, which is manifested in the fear of death. In the previous century, Arthur Schopenhauer named this longing the will to life and proclaimed that death is the problem that must confront every intellectual problem at its outset. In our end of the century, at least in America and the West, death is still denied, Schopenhauer has been forgotten, and everybody tries to paint a happy face on the world's events. Despite these conscious efforts to deny the apocalyptic import of recent political events, everyone feels that the drama of the crumbling of the Berlin Wall in 1989 reaches far beyond the mere end of the Cold War.

In 1991 America felt triumphant after its military victory over Saddam Hussein in the Persian Gulf and celebrated its civil religion with gusto. In the same year, following half a century of peace, Europe experienced wars, the conflict between Israel and the Palestinians intensified, and the Kurds were left exposed to the wrath of Hussein — to mention just three political problems that called into question President Bush's new world order. The great utopian surges, occasioned by the fall of Communism and the "end of history," were slowly scaled down to actual size. The already-familiar postindustrial problems — such as the destruction of the ozone layer, the threat of ecological and nuclear disasters, and AIDS, among many other problems that received widespread coverage in the West — reasserted themselves. The West began to realize that the fall of Communism did not mean only the triumph of democracy and capitalism over despotism. The fall of Communism did not result only in the collapse of the ruling totalitarian ideology (Bolshevik Communism), but also of the empires that owed their survival since 1945 to Communist ideology, namely, the Soviet and Yugoslav empires. The breakup of these vestiges of modern imperialism has resulted in the establishment of some twenty new nations and a series of issues that the global community will have to face, among them nuclear arms control, environmental damage, refugees, nationalism, genocide, and racism.

Our aim in this book has been to draw on cultural theorists who were instrumental in establishing sociology a century ago in order to make sense of these dramatic changes in a nonideological way. We drew deliberately upon nearly forgotten theorists because the end of ideology (from Bell 1988) released the power of their theoretical insights every bit as much as it released nationalism. In other words, the classic founding fathers of sociology seem every bit as relevant in the present fin de siècle as they were in the previous fin de siècle because nearly the same sociocultural debates are engaging humanity's collective attention now as they did then.

Centripetal Versus Centrifugal Forces

The downfall of fascism, the first major totalitarian ideology of the twentieth century, provided work for cartographers in 1945, as the map of Europe had to be redrawn. Something similar occurred in the sixties in the Southern Hemisphere when the colonial ideology crumbled; the birth of dozens of nations followed the final demise of colonial empires, especially in Africa. History repeated itself in 1991 and 1992, as the downfall of yet another totalitarian ideology, Communism, once again put the cartographers to work.

Clearly, the intellectuals who were overemphasizing the centrifugal forces of modernity that were supposed to eliminate national difference and promote globalization have been proved wrong (see Featherstone 1990). The reason is that, generally speaking, *two* processes dominate post-Communist Europe and the world. One is the centrifugal, modernist, process of unifying states and communities, exhibited by Germany in 1990 and Europe in 1992 (Bauman 1991). But the other, neglected one is the breakup of states and communities into ever-smaller units. These two opposing processes might be aptly labeled the fusion and fission theory of political development.[1] We note that as early as 1893, Emile Durkheim predicted such an antagonistic interplay of social forces involved in modernization in his still-misunderstood *Division of Labor in Society.*[2] Germany had already put the fusion theory into practice, and similar processes can be expected to take place in the foreseeable future with regard to the two Koreas, the two Yemens, the two Chinas (Taiwan and the People's Republic of China), perhaps even the two Irelands and the two Cypruses. But the fission theory applies to the

Baltic states and almost the entire former Soviet ideological empire, Canada (because of Quebec), India, Nigeria, former Czechoslovakia, and former Yugoslavia. The latent fear of the spread of fission prevented the United States and the European Community from coming to the assistance of many nations that declared their intentions to become democratic following their long ordeal with Communism. We find Oswald Spengler's theory of history to be especially helpful in explaining the West's preference for expansionist, centrifugal forces of social interaction and subsequent paralysis in the face of centripetal forces.

Nowhere in the world do ethnic boundaries and state borders coincide exactly, not even in the United States, which has had considerable problems with its Mexican border and Hispanic minority. A great many people are still searching for their own borders and nation-states, among them the Kurds and Palestinians. In contrast, there are states—complex federations and confederations—without a nation, such as Switzerland, Great Britain, and, in a way, even the United States. But it is in the Balkans that the conflict between fission and fusion, centripetal and centrifugal social forces, has been occurring with particular vigor since 1989. Historically, the Balkans have typically foreshadowed future developments, and currently is no exception. Moreover, the world generally tends to ignore the Balkans, to its ultimate chagrin. We mean that the symbolic battle between Serbia's tendency toward fusion versus Slovene, Bosnian, and Croatian fission foreshadows the forces that are now tearing apart the former Soviet Union. One of our major arguments in this book has been that the Balkan crisis of 1991 may be a watershed event that is signaling a decided shift from modernist forces that tend toward fusion to premodern or perhaps even postmodern forces that tend toward fission. These forces apply not only to issues of territory and borders but to economic, ideological, religious, and other forms of imperialism and expansion. In order to dramatize this new development, we opposed the theorists of modern social progress (Parsons, Giddens, Habermas) with the forgotten theorists of the coexistence of barbarism within modernity (Tomašić, Veblen, Spengler, Sorokin).

Habits of the Heart and the Fall of Communism

For a long time now, intellectuals and political leaders have focused mostly on the centrifugal forces of fusion that would eliminate history, nationalism, religion, and tradition. Ever since Hegel (1899), this has been the modernist dream of the Enlightenment, and its influence can be traced through Marx all the way to Fukuyama (1992). We note, however, that Hegel meant for Protestant Germany to attain the end of history and that he dismissed this possibility for the Catholics, the French, the British, and especially the Americans.[3] Paradoxically, Hegel displayed nationalism even as he proclaimed the end of nationalism! The Bolsheviks contradicted themselves similarly by furthering Russian imperialism, even as they proclaimed the end of traditional forces. Finally, we have noted that Fukuyama (1992) seems to be genuinely unaware that in proclaiming the West in general but America in particular as free of history, he is repeating the errors of Hegel and the Bolsheviks. In our cultural view of things, nationalism and tradition will never be eliminated, even in the most modern of nations, but will be transformed. For example, Bellah's (1967) concept of American civil religion captures well the modern sense of American nationalism and sense of history.

But given that fission and centripetal forces have become more noticeable in the present fin de siècle (itself a manifestation of unfinished business from the previous fin de siècle, which also had to confront nationalism), we had to account for the end point of these forces. For this reason, we resurrected Alexis de Tocqueville's concept of habits of the heart, and of habit in general, as used by William James, Oswald Spengler, and other antimodernists. This move carried significant implications for apprehending the fall of Communism. We moved out of the ideological arena represented

by Brzezinski (1989) and Fukuyama (1992) into the familiar territory of classical, fin-de-siècle sociology represented by Veblen, Durkheim, Weber, Freud, Simmel, Tönnies, and others.

The crisis and decline of Communism resulted in a number
of parallel processes that need to be distinguished analytically,
namely, the respective crises of the Soviet and Yugoslav empires,
which have led to the sudden emergence of multi-ethnic states and
the emergence of new civil religions (from Bellah 1967) rather than
the Western doctrine of liberal democracy and individual choice.
The collapse, in turn, led to an ideological and cultural vacuum for
individuals as well as collectivities. This is because in the consciousness of ordinary people, Communism was not only an ideology,
system of totalitarianism, or form of social organization; it was akin
to a religious system that was perceived to have been corrupted and
misused for personal gain by a small segment of the population.
More precisely, for the great majority of people, Communism was
a *civil religion* that was imposed upon them by force and that served
as a substitute for the extant religions (Catholicism, Orthodoxy,
Islam, Protestantism, Judaism), all of which were taken from them
by a process of forced atheism.

When the winds of historical change overwhelmed Communism as a ruling ideology, they destroyed also the existing systems
of politics and civil religion. The resultant anomic state (from Durkheim 1897) altered people's notions of identity, belonging, norma-
tive structure, even standards of what is good and evil. Moreover,
the new post-Communist trends did not lead the people to look to
the future and toward progress. Instead, they turned spontaneously toward their collective past. The historical process through
which Central and Eastern European intellectuals, politicians, and
nations are going presently is a process of searching for their lost
history. This journey into the past entailed a confrontation with
traditional habits of the heart and reflected a need to revive dor-
mant collective memories and traditions. However, these cultural
roots and identities do not lead these post-Communist individuals
and nations into a Western European *tradition* of tolerance, pan-

Europeanism, pluralism, modernism, and postmodernism (we emphasize that these constitute habits of the heart, not modernist abstractions). On the contrary, the ideological and cultural vacuum caused by the collapse of Communism led to a chaotic and sometimes violent jumble of ideologies and value systems, including populism, nationalism, neodespotism, monarchism, imperialism, racism, mysticism, anti-Semitism, and other negative aspects of tradition.

But that is only one part of the role played by traditional habits of the heart. If we break Communism and Bolshevism down into their constituent parts, namely, radical egalitarianism, totalitarianism, dictatorship, lack of freedom, and primitivism, then we notice that most of these features can be found in the political and social structures that preceded Communism. Especially in the Balkans, the tradition of absolutist government, intolerance, imperialism, and general backwardness precedes Communism. To emphasize this point—which tends to be neglected by Western, modernist, intellectuals who are not sufficiently mindful of cultural theories—we attempted to revivify the theories of Dinko Tomašić (1948b, 1953). More than any other political analyst of Communism, Tomašić recognized the authoritarian traditions that *preceded* Communism and that might be extremely difficult to overcome now that Communism appears to have collapsed. Thus, an important contribution of our approach to this political discourse is the observation that the cultural roots of Communism have not been destroyed simply because Communism has been discredited as an ideology and economic and political system. It is still very possible for Communism to transform itself into a new totalitarian and brutal system of oppression, and we have argued that this is precisely what has occurred in Serbia.

In sum, without a cultural approach that stresses the importance of habits of the heart, a realistic understanding of the processes at work in post-Communist lands is impossible to achieve. Beyond question, it is already evident that the abstract theories of capitalist utopia and the end of history are being proved wrong by the resurgence of history in the Balkans and the southern fringes of the former Soviet Empire (Ryan 1992).

The Rebirth of History

To repeat, one of our major objectives has been to suggest that contrary to Fukuyama's (1992) excessively optimistic thesis concerning the end of history,[4] history has reasserted itself in the Balkans. In particular, the aim of the Balkan War of 1991 was for Serbia to defeat or conquer Croatia, wholly or in part, for the sake of reasons that Fukuyama declared nonexistent,[5] namely, imperialism, gratuitous aggression, and prejudice. It is a war that is motivated by an atavistic tendency for territorial expansion and a collective obsession with conquest, destruction, and domination.

At least initially, none of these factors were obvious to the West, which was smitten by its optimistic theories of what post-Communism would be like. Instead of responding enthusiastically to Slovenia's and Croatia's democratic declarations of independence, the West responded with ambivalence because it felt threatened by the forces of fission. Instead of seeing through the Serbian propaganda of waging a war on its neighbors in order to protect its minority living elsewhere—the same fictitious motives that were used by the Nazis in their conquests—the West was seduced by Serbia's modernist language of seeking to preserve the Yugoslav federation. The West had forgotten, at least temporarily, that the Communist Yugoslav federation was maintained by force and dominated by Serbs and Montenegrins. Here again, however, Tomašić (1948b) had already analyzed and predicted such developments.

In order to avoid the charge of being partisan, we relied on a series of Helsinki Watch Committee reports on the Yugoslav crisis. We shall review here the Helsinki Watch (1991a) version of the events that led to the war between the Croats and Serbs in 1991. Tudjman was elected as the president of Croatia in May of 1990. "With the election of Tudjman's HDZ party, many former communist bureaucrats—many of whom were Serbs—were replaced with Tudjman's appointees" (p. 2).[6] Soon after, "Tudjman acceded and drafted a plan for cultural autonomy for ethnic Serbs," but "the Serbs demanded political autonomy, including control over local police stations in areas where Serbs constitute a majority" (p. 2). In March 1991 "Serbian insurgents occupied the police station in Pakrac and tried to take over the Plitvice National Park on Croatia."[7] Fighting began to increase along the border of Croatia and Serbia as well as in Bosnia-Hercegovina. On June 25, 1991, Slovenia and Croatia declared their independence, and thereafter the fighting intensified. "Croatian authorities have played a defensive role in most cases and resisted Serbian military advances." However, the Yugoslav federal army, "whose officer corps is predominantly Serbian and whose interests lie in the preservation of a Yugoslav state, has continued to intervene in the conflict," and "these interventions have had the effect of preserving territorial gains made by the Serbs in Croatia" (p. 3).

In May of 1991, Serbia launched an attack on Croatia with the support of the Yugoslav federal army, which is a Soviet-style army consisting of 2,000 tanks, 400 warplanes, a 300-ship navy, 10,000 pieces of artillery, and some 300,000 troops. In addition to capturing territory, the Serbian-backed armies attacked and destroyed Croatian cultural landmarks as well as symbols of Christianity and Western culture in general, including churches, graveyards, theaters, museums, and historical treasures. It was a war on Croatian as well as Western civil religions in that the Serbs destroyed portions of Dubrovnik, Šibenik, and other world-historical treasures that had been left intact by Napoleon, Hitler, and Mussolini—even by the Turks. The fact that the Serbs and Montenegrins took aim primarily at civilian and cultural targets exposes the falsehood that they acted to protect their minority rights. According to Helsinki Watch (1991b:3):

> Serbs living in Croatia feel threatened by the resurrection of Croatian nationalism—both within the Croatian government and among the general populace. The Serbs claim that such fervent national-

ism is a prelude to the resurrection of the World War II Nazi puppet state under which thousands of Serbs were killed. They believe
that an independent Croatia would be a fascist state . . . they do not
want to live in areas where the traditional Croatian flag flies, claiming that thousands of Serbs were massacred under that flag during
World War II. They view traditional Croatian songs as fascist, anti-
Serbian and anti-Yugoslav.

We note that the conflict in the Balkans was sparked by issues pertaining to culture — in particular, over civil religion. For example, the alleged persecution of the Serbian minority in Croatia
had to do with the use of the Cyrillic alphabet. The Serbs "claim
that they do not have the right to use their Cyrillic alphabet and
language throughout Croatia; they reject Croatian as the official
language of Croatia" (p. 4). But Helsinki Watch points out that the
Croatian constitution of December 1990 guarantees equal civil and
political rights to all ethnic minorities; furthermore, "Article XXI
of the Constitution expressly grants the right of the Serbian population to use both the Latin and Cyrillic alphabets in areas where
Serbs constitute a majority" (p. 4).

The aims and methods used by the Serbs in the war illustrate Tomašić's (1948b) central claim that Dinaric and Eastern cultures value brute force, supremacy, passion, and conquest. The Serbs
had hoped to push their own borders and culture further west by
means of war, including the destruction of all the material evidence
of the existence of Croatian and Western European culture. They
hoped to gain access to the Adriatic Sea as well as the oil fields in
Slavonia and the fertile land in Baranja. According to Helsinki Watch
(1991a:4): "The position of many Serbian insurgents is: 'If the Croats
want to secede from Yugoslavia, good riddance to them. But if they
secede, they will not take one Serb, or any land on which a Serb
lives, with them.' Other Serbs have called for a 'Greater Serbia,' in
which Serbia would rule all of present-day Yugoslavia, except for
Zagreb (the Croatian capital) and its environs, and Slovenia."

Clearly, these imperialist tactics and objectives hark back to
the Europe of the first half of the twentieth century. Modern forms

of domination, even exploitation, have long ceased to be based on military force, war, and the conquest of territory. They are based instead on technological, economic, and scientific supremacy. The territorial instinct or a fascination with territory is a basic feature of the nomadic, barbaric consciousness discussed by Veblen, Tomašić, Spengler, and other cultural theorists.

The Serbian intellectual, military, and political elite knew that because of their backward economic and technological state of development relative to Croatia and Slovenia, supremacy could be achieved only through seizing power and imposing military force. In this sense, we attempted to draw a parallel between the historical German and contemporary Serbian fascination with territory and imperialism vis-à-vis the analyses of World War I by Spengler and Tomašić.[8] The German victory in the war of 1870 led to the defeat of 1918, and later to the disaster of 1945. When the German people gave up their territorial fascination and military imperialism, they became a cultural and technological leader in Europe and the rest of the world.[9] Similarly, Serbia's old-fashioned barbarism cannot bring victory or prosperity in the long run. Eventually, it will bring catastrophic ruin, as it did for the Germans. But long before this occurs, there is a danger that the destruction of its neighbors will set back the West's hopes for the modernization and democratization of the Balkans. The war has had and will continue to have a devastating effect on the economy, health, and morale of peoples in the Balkans who yearn sincerely for democracy.

In the cultural sense, a Western European consciousness hardly exists at all in Serbia, confined as it is among certain urban intellectuals, primarily in Belgrade.[10] While Croatian cultural history was influenced heavily by Roman Catholicism and the Austro-Hungarian Empire, the history of Serbian culture is based on the principle of Balkan particularism—the myth and cult of Serbian uniqueness and superiority. For example, Serbia insisted on maintaining the Cyrillic alphabet among its minority living in Croatia, even though Serbia is the only European nation to use this outmoded alphabet. It refused to admit its minority status within Croatia, even though Serbs constitute only 11.5 percent of Croatia's population. But "the Serbs reject their relegation to minority status" because they see themselves as a special people who liberated Croatia and the Balkans (Helsinki Watch Committee 1991a:4). This is one instance among many of Serbia's intolerance and cultural narcissism relative to all other cultures. It should be noted that Croatia granted its Serbian minority the right to use the Cyrillic alphabet, which did not appease them (Helsinki Watch Committee 1991a:4). In a similar vein, Serbia destroyed all material evidence of the cultural presence of the Turks on Serbian territory, a presence that lasted almost five hundred years, and engaged in a brutal suppression of the Muslim *majority* population in Kosovo (Helsinki Watch Committee 1990). For example, not a single mosque has survived in Belgrade, which used to boast two hundred mosques in the mid-nineteenth century.

The European traditions of the Renaissance, baroque, Art Nouveau, and modernism never took root in Serbian culture. Serbian art and culture has been confined mainly to the Serbian Orthodox church, which retained its independence even during Turkish rule. As recently as the 1980s, eminent and influential Serbian intellectuals have been promoting xenophobia, intolerance, and cultural aggression among the population. The induced sense of collective ethnic peril coupled with the cultural narcissism described above led to a strong nationalist movement that was exploited by Slobodan Milošević. This same movement has been responsible for repression and human rights abuses against the Muslim minority in Kosovo, the brief conflict in Slovenia, and the tragic war in Croatia and Bosnia-Hercegovina.

While the armies of the former Soviet satellites Poland, Hungary, and former Czechoslovakia seem to have accepted the process of democratization with considerable tolerance, this is not the case with Soviet and Yugoslav federal armies, which have experienced the end of Communism as the end of the world. We have appealed to Tomašić's cultural theories in order to try to make sense of Soviet and Yugoslav tendencies toward hegemony and imperialism by suggesting that these two armies operate on the basis of the Ural and

Dinaric cultural mind-sets, respectively. For example, in the period of transition from Communism, the Yugoslav federal army and government were offered every modern formula for compromise by the European Community as well as the Croatians and Slovenes, including a commonwealth of independent states, an asymmetrical federation, and a confederation. None of them was deemed satisfactory. Placing their trust solely in the use of brute force, the Serbian-led federal government of Yugoslavia chose violence, war, and crime. In Fukuyama's lanugage, it chose "history." Paradoxically, it is now on the verge of civilizational decline, of being ostracized from Europe.

At this point we have returned, full circle, to Fukuyama's fascinating thesis that humanity has reached the end of history and will no longer tolerate the sort of imperialism that Serbia displayed in the war that began in 1991 against its neighbors. Fukuyama is partly right, in that the modern world does espouse the values of human rights, democracy, pluralism, and peaceful coexistence. Yet, the world also permitted Serbia to inflict terrible damage upon Croatia and Bosnia-Hercegovina, whereas it stood up to Saddam Hussein's imperialistic adventure in Kuwait. We have attempted to show that something is not completely right with Fukuyama's thesis, although in this book, we are less concerned with analyzing the West's ambivalence in response to the latest Balkan crisis than with the cultural origins of the return of history in post-Communist lands. Nevertheless, we did touch briefly on the reasons for the ambivalence of the Western response to Croatian, Bosnian, and Slovene self-determination from a cultural vantage point.

Drawing upon Veblen and Spengler, we noted that the Western tradition is also a blend of barbaric and Christian values, self-interest as well as compassion. At various junctures in the history of the West, one or the other pole of this dualism tends to dominate over the other. At the present time, from the perspective of the post-Communist lands, the West is espousing democratic values but offering minimal moral and material assistance to formerly Communist nations. Moreover, efforts to export "pure capitalism" (which does not exist in this pure state even in the West) to post-Communist lands has thus far resulted in great hardship for the Poles, Russians, and others. There exists the possibility that many post-Communist lands will conclude that the West is cruel and indifferent, a sentiment already expressed in Slovene, Bosnian, and Croatian media. This perception will certainly not aid in the spread of Western liberal democratic ideals.

The Croatian nation displayed a naive faith in the metaphors surrounding its understanding of Europe, of the West, and even of the United States as the best model of democracy. It placed an uncritical trust in the West to prevent and stop the war that erupted in 1991, to grant instant and unconditional diplomatic recognition to its declaration of independence, and to offer leadership and assistance in the difficult transition from Communism to democracy. Croatian naïveté was perhaps more extreme than that of other post-Communist nations, but in general the newly liberated nations have been disillusioned by a West that preaches the end of history and the virtues of liberal democracy, while in fact it acts on the basis of self-interest and maintenance of the status quo.

We drew upon the works of David Riesman, Christopher Lasch, Robert Bellah, and others who seem to have been inspired by Tocqueville's dark predictions concerning American and Western freedom, namely, that it could degenerate into narcissism and selfishness. Indeed, the West in general and the United States in particular expressed minimal curiosity about the post-Communist drama unfolding in Europe, in line with Riesman's (1980a) observation that narcissism dulls curiosity. Western media coverage devoted far more attention to domestic issues than to a deep understanding of one of the most dramatic events of the twentieth century—the fall of Communism and its consequences. For example, as late as March 1992, former president Richard Nixon (1992a) pointed out that none of the U.S. presidential candidates had anything to say about foreign policy toward post-Communist nations.

Thus, the newly liberated post-Communist nations had to choose between remnants of the old, power-seeking order that had been enshrined in Communism versus a decadent, narcissistic Western culture that celebrated the virtues of liberal democracy even as it did little to promote it. Concepts such as freedom, justice, democracy, and human rights no longer hold the power to inspire faith because they had all been subjected to ideological manipulation. The Communists in Yugoslavia and elsewhere talked about democratic centralism, the rule of the working class, equal rights for women and the oppressed, even democractic self-management. All this talk masked horrifying oppression. Now that Communism deception has been exposed, the West uses the vocabulary of liberal democracy, the end of history, and the free market in an effort to impose still another socially engineered system upon post-Communist nations. We have pointed out the irony that like the Bolsheviks, Fukuyama (1992) even relies upon Marx and Hegel as his philosophical scaffolding for promoting liberal democracy. The Eastern Europeans have had all the Marx and Hegel they can take. It is not at all evident that the Western model of liberal democracy is universal or that the Eastern Europeans and former Soviets will adopt it.

For example, from the cultural vantage point of Eastern Europe, there exist a number of alternatives to the Western and particularly American models of liberal democracy and free-market institutions. Japan, Korea, Taiwan, Singapore, and Hong Kong have achieved almost instant modernization. Spain is frequently discussed in Eastern Europe as an example of a country that made the transition from fascism to democracy without losing its tradition and heritage.

In general, the concepts "post-Communism" and "end of history" are theoretically and politically empty abstractions. "Post-Communism" merely denotes a segment of time that in the history of Eastern and Central Europe follows the fall of Communism. That is why it has become, so to speak, a blank page upon which history is being written again. Each and every post-Communist nation will find its own unique path to democracy and capitalism on the basis of its own habits of the heart. Indeed, there exists evidence that this is already occurring, if one compares the differences among former East Germany, Poland, former Czechoslovakia, Croatia, and Slovenia, among others (Stark 1992). In sum, democracy and free-market institutions do not exist as abstractions, except in the minds of some leading Western intellectuals. These ideas are filtered and refracted through a nation's tradition and cultural outlook.

Returning to the Balkan crisis, one can see that Croatia will have to resolve a number of difficult issues in the aftermath of the war that began in 1991, including the return of refugees, the rebuilding of a devastated economy, the reestablishment of communication, the investigation and punishment of war crimes, the building of a defense force, and dealing with its homeless, disabled, and dead. In general, it will have to modernize and join the rest of Europe in the context of its cultural heritage, its own civil religion, and the added burden of the consequnces of the war. While other Western European nations were going through the process of social transformation from absolutism and early capitalism into modern, postindustrial, and even postmodern liberal societies, Croatia and most other newly liberated nations were wasting historical time "developing" an autistic form of Communism and self-management. It is interesting to note how rarely such realistic handicaps enter into Western and American discourse concerning the future of post-Communism.

The fundamental building blocks of modern, Western societies are the cult of the individual (from Durkheim 1893) and the notion of human rights. But instead of fostering the individual, the doctrine of individualism, and the notion of human rights, Communism merely transformed one form of autocracy and authoritarianism into another. For us, this is the seminal value of Tomašić's cultural analysis of Communism. We would modify Brzezinski's (1989) thesis that Communism died to the effect that Communism was merely the metamorphosis of a bad aspect to Slavic cultures that is still operative in post-Communist lands. It could very well undergo still another metamorphosis, as it did in Serbia, Georgia, and some of the other southern fringes of the former Soviet Empire.

Communism transformed feudal collectivism—which glorifies the sense of tribal, communal, or local belonging as opposed to universalism—into new forms of collective consciousness, namely, the sense of belonging to the working classes, the slogans "brotherhood and unity" and, ultimately, "vanguard of the working class," or the League of Communists. The fall of Communism and the outbreak of hostilities in the Balkans and some portions of the former Soviet Union have automatically transformed these forms of collective consciousness (from Durkheim) into a nationalistic collective consciousness. Nationalism erupted almost as soon as Communism fell.

In this book, we have argued for the need to distinguish between good and bad forms of nationalism and others aspects of culture. We realize that this move is problematic from the perspective of cultural relativism, which denies absolute standards of right and wrong, or good and evil. Without entering into a long philosophical debate with the cultural relativists and extreme postmodernists, we drew upon Tocqueville's own straightforward but somewhat neglected distinction between the bad America that exterminated the Indians and established slavery versus the good America of freedom and democracy. Our point is that no serious thinker today could possibly defend slavery or the extermination of the Indians, so that the cultural relativist position, in this regard, is a moot point. Similarly, it is impossible to justify or rationalize the Serbian attacks against unarmed civilians and the malicious destruction of culture. These acts constitute bad nationalism, pure and simple.

The danger is that all of the post-Communist nations might develop these negative forms of nationalism. For example, even Croatia, which characterizes itself primarily as a victim in the war that began in 1991, displays some dangerous tendencies in its nationalism. The party that won the 1990 elections in Croatia—the Croatian Democratic Union, or HDZ—has been found guilty of human rights abuses, censoring opposition, restricting freedom of the press, and resorting to coercion and force rather than dialogue and pluralism (Helsinki Watch Committee 1992a).

In sum, our cultural explanation of post-Communism emphasizes that its trajectory will involve the interplay of peaceable as well
as power-seeking habits of the heart. The desired triumph of the
peaceable, democratic tradition will be aided by recognition of the
fact that it is a *historical tradition* that must be nurtured at the same
time that autocratic cultural forces are exposed and avoided. We
propose that this awareness of cultural forces is as necessary in the
West as in post-Communist lands. Adherence to the dogma that history has come to an end exposes the West to the foolishness of per-
mitting history to repeat itself.

Notes

1. For an opposing view, see Mikhael Gorbachev's (1992) op-ed in the *New York Times*. For the sake of continuity, consider Gorbachev (1986a, 1986b, 1987).

2. To be sure, Fukuyama (1989, 1990, 1991, 1992) has been modifying his position in response to critics. Nevertheless, his latest position is that "the ideal of liberal democracy could not be improved on" and that "religion, nationalism, and a people's complex of ethical habits and customs (more broadly 'culture') have traditionally been interpreted as obstacles to the establishment of successful democratic political institutions and free-market economies" (1992:xix). He adds immediately, "But the truth is considerably more complicated." For a critique of Fukuyama, see Ryan (1992). For an excellent discussion of the "end of history" thesis in a postmodern context, see Rosenau (1992). For discussions of various aspects of Hegelian philosophy and utopianism, see Cooper (1984), Holsti (1991), Molnar (1967), and Peet (1991).

3. For example, an editorial in the *Wall Street Journal* on December 31, 1991, entitled " A Year of Freedom" concluded that "so far, however, only the wild-eyed optimists have proved correct."

4. For a critique of the optimistic position that uses recent empirical evidence, see Stark (1992). See also Amitai Etzioni's (1988, 1991a, 1991b, 1991c) critiques of so-called classical economic theory. Various other aspects of exporting capitalism are treated by Craycraft (1991), Ferfila (1991), Forman (1991), Hankiss (1990), and Hollander (1988).

5. For example, see Anderson (1992).

6. For articles published in the *American Journal of Sociology*, see Tomašić (1941, 1946, 1948a). In the *American Sociological Review*, see

Tomašić (1951). For a complete listing of Tomašić's publications, see Stulhofer (1992).

7. All of these authors are treated in *World and I* 3, no. 9 (Sept. 1988): 544–678, a special edition edited by Lawrence Criner.

8. Zygmunt Bauman, *Intimations of Postmodernity* (London: Routledge, 1992). This work needs to be read in the context of Bauman's (1987, 1989, 1991) earlier works on modernity and postmodernity. See also the review by Anthony Giddens (1992). We cannot do justice to the connections between postmodernism and post-Communism, which is treated at greater length by the authors elsewhere (Meštrović, Goreta, and Letica 1993). See also Featherstone (1988), Kroker and Cook (1986), and Kroker and Kroker (1991).

9. As argued by Dinko Tomašić, *Personality and Culture in Eastern European Politics* (New York: George Stewart, 1948), and *The Impact of Russian Culture on Soviet Communism* (Glencoe, Ill.: Free Press, 1953).

10. For example, Spengler (1926:26) writes: "Rome, with its rigorous realism—uninspired, barbaric, disciplined, practical, Protestant, Prussian—will always give us, working as we must by analogy, the key to understanding our own future."

11. Stephen Kalberg (1987) offers one of the best recent analyses of the German tendency to regard "culture" as superior to the Anglo-American and French notions of "civilization." This distinction was especially important to Sigmund Freud, Ferdinand Tönnies, Oswald Spengler, and Norbert Elias, among others.

12. Spengler (1926:32) elaborates: "The Romans were barbarians who did not precede but closed a great development. Unspiritual, unphilosophical, devoid of art, clannish to the point of brutality, aiming relentlessly at tangible successes . . . in a word, Greek soul—Roman intellect; and this antithesis is the differentia between culture and civilization."

13. Or when it is cited, as in the case of Fukuyama (1992:322–26), it is cited incorrectly as a one-sided glorification of the American experiment in democracy. Anyone who has read Tocqueville (1845) knows that such an element is present. Tocqueville, however, was also a critic of American democracy, making some very pessimistic prophecies concerning its eventual outcome as well.

14. Taken from the syllabus of David Riesman's course at Harvard, Social Sciences 136, Character and Social Structure in America. See also Riesman (1953, 1954, 1964, 1976, 1977, 1980a, 1980b, 1981, 1990) as well as Riesman and Riesman (1967).

15. See, for example, the recent criticisms of this work made by Bau-

man (1991). Even if Adorno et al. *The Authoritarian Personality* (1950) is flawed empirically, its central, theoretical premise—that political movements are rooted in culture, including the family and religion—seems basically sound.

16. For example, see Scrinton (1988).

17. See, for example, Banac and Buskovitch (1983).

18. In contradistinction to Fukuyama's "end of history."

19. Note the continued relevance of Tocqueville's observation that in Europe, newspapers are full of heated arguments and editorials, whereas in America, three-quarters of the newspaper is filled with advertisements ([1845] 1945:185). It has been our experience that even East European newspapers offer far more in-depth political coverage than most American newspapers.

20. See, for example, Adorno's *Culture Industry* (1991).

CHAPTER 2

1. This claim is documented in Helsinki Watch (1982, 1990, 1991a, 1991b, 1992a, 1992b).

2. David Riesman wrote to Meštrović in a letter dated March 9, 1992, pertaining to this possibility: "I have often wondered what might have happened if the South could have separated from the North without a civil war. Would there have been a feasible boundary? Would there have developed guerrilla warfare? I have only occasionally wondered what would have happened if the English had come to the aid of the South. Even in my counter-factual moments I find it hard to envisage the South occupying New England, for example. I do not think that New England remains the 'beacon' of cultural values for the United States. I doubt if there is such a beacon."

3. In particular, Raymond Gastil (1971) argues that as far back as records have been kept in the United States, the South has always exhibited much higher homicide rates than the North. He traced the migration patterns of Yankees and southerners to the West and found correlations of murder rates with dominance of southerners. Gastil's thesis is highly controversial, and there have been many efforts to disprove it. But no final resolution of the issues that he raises has been offered yet. We use his study only to suggest that Tocqueville's theoretical explanation of the empirical facts that concern Gastil and others is worth taking seriously. It is beyond the scope of the present discussion to enter any further into this matter.

4. For example, see Anderson (1992) and Tagliabue (1991), among the many others who argued that the republics that wanted independence from Serbia were too small or too poor to survive, or that the breakup of

the former Yugoslavia was otherwise undesirable; see also Barro (1991), Gagnon (1991), Glenny (1992), Kaplan (1991), Lendvai (1991), and Viorst (1991). See also Richard Nixon's (1991, 1992b) counterarguments. For example, Nixon noted that breakaway Slovenia was larger than over fifty other nations in the United Nations. Consider also Murvar's (1982) and Tudjman's (1981) compelling argument that Croatia and the other breakaway republics were actually submerged nations.

5. In this regard, Kosovo might be regarded as the Alamo of the South Slavs. But what a difference from the Alamo of the Americans as a tourist trap, described by Baudrillard (1986:2). See also Baudrillard (1988, 1990, 1991) and the fine recent analysis of Baudrillard's importance by Mike Gane (1991).

6. An important ambiguity emerged in the discussion, namely, whether it is meaningful for Bellah and others to refer to contemporary American habits of the heart, given the alleged transitions from culture to civilization, gemeinschaft to gesellschaft, and heart to mind, among others, that have supposedly accompanied modernization. Our intent has been to expose this ambiguity, not resolve it. For the sake of context, it is important to trace the development of Bellah's implicit and explicit concept of American civil religion (Bellah 1967, 1970, 1972, 1981, 1989).

7. The *Wall Street Journal,* February 21, 1992. It should go without saying that some Yugoslavs desire peace and democracy.

8. For one example among many, see *Hrvatski Tjednik,* December 23, 1991.

CHAPTER 3

1. For example, see Karan's (1974a, 1974b, 1977, 1983) many studies of blood vengeance. Other authors replicate many of Tomašić's findings without mentioning him directly, among them Bakovic (1985), Humphrey (1989), Edynak et al. (1976), Pecjak (1992), Petak (1974), Pilon (1992), and Stojsavljević (1974). Thurow (1991a, 1991b) demonstrates how traditional autocracy persists, despite so-called democratic reforms. Golitsyn (1984) would have one consider that all apparent reform in the former Soviet Union is a deceitful cover for the persistence of antidemocratic tendencies.

2. The Serbian rationalization for these and other actions is that Hitler and Tito drew up the present-day borders, which put Serbia at a disadvantage, and that wherever one finds Serbs living, there one finds Serbia. It is not our intention to delve into the history of various borders in former Yugoslavia. Let us suppose, for the sake of discussion, that the Serbs are right that the borders are not accurate or fair. The important point, from our theoretical perspective, is that the Serbian government did not attempt

to negotiate new borders. Rather, it seized territory in the guise of protecting its Serbian minority in neighboring republics from possible genocide. We note that Hitler, as well as other dictators, used similar arguments to justify territorial expansion.

3. Burns went on to explain: "By Chetniks, the Gorazde commander meant the irregular Serbian forces who have played a major role in the Bosnian fighting and who have claimed the name of the Serbian guerillas who fought the Nazis in Bosnia during World War II. The name is used with pride by the Serbian fighters, but as an epithet by those fighting for the Bosnian government" (p. A-4).

4. Tomašić seems to be using the zero-sum concept in an unorthodox way. In Western usage, this concept refers to a situation in which one actor's losses are exactly another actor's gains.

5. However, all such East-West comparisons are ambiguous. One could argue that capitalism is a zero-sum phenomenon because what the proleteriat loses, the capitalists gain. If Tomašić is correct that the Dinaric types tend to interpret situations in zero-sum terms, then it seems to follow that their soial character should be conducive to capitalism. In fact, pure capitalism is not taking hold in former Yugoslavia. It could well be the case that capitalism, as it is practiced in the West, is more complex than the ideal-type capitalism that is being exported to Eastern Europe. For example, Thorstein Veblen (1943) argued that capitalism contains some barbaric cultural elements that are at odds with the peaceable and democratic traits with which it is typically associated.

6. In a letter to Meštrović, March 11, 1991.

CHAPTER 4

1. For more on the connections between Freud and Veblen, see Schneider (1948).

2. However, this view should not be attributed to Kalberg. It is discussed by David Riesman (1953) and is obviously highly controversial. We do not necessarily agree with Veblen but do certainly find his view intriguing.

CHAPTER 5

1. Here again we only touch on a vast discussion that Meštrović (1992) and Meštrović, Goreta, and Letica (1993) treat elsewhere at length. For the sake of context, Fromm's other works need to be considered (1947, 1950, 1964). We feel that one of Erich Fromm's most insightful critics is C. G. Schoenfeld (1962, 1966, 1968, 1974, 1988, 1991).

2. The president of the North American Schopenhauer Society,

David Cartwright, offers insightful discussions of this point (1984, 1987, 1988a, 1988b, 1991).

3. We find it interesting that she is never referred to as the Bosnian Madonna, but always as the Croatian Madonna, even though, technically, she appears in Bosnia-Hercegovina.

4. It is as if Spengler and Weber address two halves of a giant puzzle without ever noticing that it needs to be put together: Weber ignores the Marian, Gothic preamble to Calvin, whereas Spengler assumes, with incredible naïveté, that patriarchy simply builds on matriarchy.

5. By "feminine," Spengler was referring to the classical philosophy of live and let live and in this sense referred to Hellenic culture as feminine.

6. An editorial in the *Wall Street Journal* of September 10, 1992, hinted at this connection: "State-run media outlets across the Arab world have likened the Serbian assaults on Sarajevo to a 'Christian crusade.' . . . Clerics have used the situation to stoke anti-Western resentments, with *Al-Riad*, the Saudi newspaper calling the Bosnian war a 'prelude to the war between Islam and the West.' . . . The Yugoslav breakup has been a humiliation for the West, so there is little ground upon which to object to others trying to broker a solution. . . . The final lesson of this Muslim intervention should be a reminder that the Yugoslav chaos could escalate in ways we might not like" (p. A-14).

CHAPTER 6

1. In "Go Forth and Unify," *London Economist*, October 6, 1990.

2. For example, Durkheim ([1893] 1933:130) writes: "There are, here, two contrary forces, one centripetal, the other centrifugal, which cannot flourish at the same time." The centripetal forces are characteristic of "primitive" societies held together by "mechanical solidarity," whereas the centrifugal forces are characteristic of "advanced" societies held together by "organic solidarity" and an advanced division of labor. However, in Durkheim's theory, the progress of the division of labor does not entail a complete dissolution of earlier, centripetal forces. Thus, he writes on the next page, "Even in the exercise of our occupation, we conform to usages, to practices which are common to our whole professional brotherhood. But, even in this instance, the yoke that we submit to is much less heavy than when society completely controls us." For a fuller discussion, see Meštrović (1988).

3. For example, Hegel writes ([1899] 1965:419): "The Reformation originated in Germany, and struck firm root only in the purely German nations . . . even South Germany has only partially adopted the Reformation."

He writes further that his discussion brings him "to the last stage in History, our world, our own time" (p. 442). He then proceeds to criticize the French Revolution and the French for not realizing the theoretical implications of freedom, because "the French are hot-headed" (p. 444). But, "It was the Protestant World itself which advanced so far in Thought as to realize the absolute culmination of Self-Consciousness." He adds, "An intellectual principle was thus discovered to serve as a basis for the State—one which does not, like previous principles, belong to the sphere of opinion" (p. 445). The effects of the strong German State are well known, and one is at a loss as to how Fukuyama (1992) can argue that liberalism can be derived from Hegel.

4. We shall repeat our claim, made in chapter 1, that Fukuyama's thesis is actually more complex than it first appears and that he has modified his position several times since 1989. Nevertheless, Fukuyama (1990:20) does claim that "nationalism has been a threat to liberalism historically" and fails to see that Western and American forms of liberalism are "nationalistic" in their own ways, as forms of civil religion.

5. To be sure, Fukuyama modified his 1989 optimism in 1990, 1991, and 1992. For a discussion, see Rosenau (1992).

6. It is worth comparing this practice with similar practices by American, French, and Western governments that win elections. While the Communists were in power, they controlled Croatian bureaucracy, and more Serbians joined the Communist party than Croatians.

7. According to Helsinki Watch (1991a:4): "While conceding that they held a disproportionate number of high-level positions while Croatia was under communist rule, they assert that they are now being dismissed from their jobs because of their national origin. . . . Under the communist regime, Serbs made up the vast majority of the Croatian police force. Now they comprise less than 25 percent." Compare this situation with similar issues in the United States concerning representation of minorities on police forces.

8. One of the most striking similarities between imperialist Germany and Serbia is that both perceived themselves as liberators of the peoples and lands they subjugated. This was Hitler's rationalization, for example. According to Helsinki Watch (1991a:4): "Some Serbs claim that the Serbian people have contributed much to the freedom of the Croats because the Serbs liberated the Croats from the horrors of fascism during World War II. As liberators, the Serbs believe that the Croats are indebted to them and that the relegation of Serbs to a minority status denigrates their contribution to Croatian society."

9. We acknowledge a similar discussion by Stanko Lasić in unpublished remarks.

10. Note that Slobodan Milošević was elected primarily by the rural population of Serbia.

References

Adams, H. [1901] 1983. The Dynamo and the Virgin. In *The Education of Henry Adams*, pp. 1068–75. New York: Viking.

Adorno, T. W. 1991. *The Culture Industry*. London: Routledge.

Adorno, T. W.; Frenkel-Bruswik, E.; Levinson, D.; and Sanford, R. N. 1950. *The Authoritarian Personality*. New York: Harper.

Anderson, D. 1992. A Diplomat Explains Yugoslavia. *Wall Street Journal*, February 21.

Arendt, H. 1962. *The Origins of Totalitarianism*. New York: Meridian.

Augustin, D. R. 1974. Traditional Thinking. *Sociologija* 16 (1): 73–86.

Bachofen, J. J. [1861] 1967. *Myth, Religion, and Mother Right*. Princeton: Princeton University Press.

Bailey, R. B. 1958. *Sociology Faces Pessimism: A Study of European Sociological Thought amidst a Fading Optimism*. The Hague: Martinus Nijhoff.

Baković, T. 1985. *Depresivni Optimizam Crnogoraca*. Zagreb: Jugoart.

Banac, I., and Buskovitch, P. 1983. *The Nobility in Russia and Eastern Europe*. Columbus, Ohio: Slavica Press.

Barro, R. J. 1991. Small Is Beautiful. *Wall Street Journal*, October 11, p. A-11.

Baudrillard, J. 1981. *Critique of the Political Economy of the Sign*. Translated by C. Levin. St. Louis: Telos Press.

———. 1986. *America*. London: Verso.

———. 1988. *Selected Writings*. Stanford: Stanford University Press.

———. 1990. *Seduction*. New York: St. Martin's Press.

———. 1991. The Reality Gulf. *Guardian*, January 11, p. 25.

Bauman, Z. 1987. *Legislators and Interpreters: On Modernity, Post-Modernity, and Intellectuals.* Ithaca, N.Y.: Cornell University Press.

———. 1989. *Modernity and the Holocaust.* Ithaca, N.Y.: Cornell University Press.

———. 1991. *Modernity and Ambivalence.* Ithaca, N.Y.: Cornell University Press.

———. 1992. *Intimations of Postmodernity.* London: Routledge.

Bell, D. 1976. *The Cultural Contradictions of Capitalism.* New York: Basic Books.

———. 1988. *The End of Ideology.* Cambridge: Harvard University Press.

Bellah, R. N. 1967. Civil Religion in America. *Daedalus* 96:1–21.

———. 1970. *Beyond Belief.* New York: Harper & Row.

———. 1972. *Emile Durkheim on Morality and Society.* Chicago: University of Chicago Press.

———. 1981. Democratic Culture or Authoritarian Capitalism? *Society* 18 (6): 41–50.

———. 1989. Reply to Mathisen. *Sociological Analysis* 50 (2): 149.

Bellah, R. N.; Madsen, R.; Sullivan, W. M.; Swidler, A.; and Tipton, S. M. 1985. *Habits of the Heart.* Berkeley: University of California Press.

———. 1991. *The Good Society.* New York: Alfred A. Knopf.

Berman, H. J. 1991. Law and Religion in the Development of a World Order. *Sociological Analysis* 52 (1): 27–36.

Bloom, A. 1987. *The Closing of the American Mind.* New York: Simon & Schuster.

Botić, I., and Djureković, S. 1983. *Yugoslavia in Crisis: The Political and Economic Dimensions.* New York: Croatian National Congress.

Braaten, J. 1991. *Habermas's Critical Theory of Society.* Albany: State University of New York Press.

Brucan, S. 1989. *World Socialism at the Crossroads.* New York: Praeger.

————. 1990. *Pluralism and Social Conflict.* New York: Praeger.

Bryant, C. G., and Jary, D. 1991. *Giddens' Theory of Structuration: A Critical Appreciation.* London: Routledge.

Brzezinski, Z. 1989. *The Grand Failure: The Birth and Death of Communism in the Twentieth Century.* New York: Scribner's.

Cartwright, D. 1984. Kant, Schopenhauer, and Nietzsche on the Morality of Pity. *Journal of the History of Ideas* 45 (1): 83–98.

————. 1987. Kant's View of the Moral Significance of Kindhearted Emotions and the Moral Insignificance of Kant's View. *Journal of Value Inquiry* 21:291–304.

————. 1988. Schopenhauer's Axiological Analysis of Character. *Revue International de Philosophie* 42:18–36.

————. 1988b. Schopenhauer's Compassion and Nietzsche's Pity. *Schopenhauer Jahrbuch* 69:557–67.

————. 1991. Reversing Silenus' Wisdom. *Nietzsche Studien* 20:301–13.

Caute, D. 1988. *The Fellow-Travellers: Intellectual Friends of Communism.* New Haven: Yale University Press.

Clark, J.; Modgil, C.; and Modgil, S. 1990. *Anthony Giddens; Consensus and Controversy.* London: Falmer Press.

Clemens, W. C. 1989. Perestroika Needs a Work Ethic to Work. *Wall Street Journal,* December 5, p. A-12.

Cohen, P. J. 1992. History Misappropriated. *Midstream* 38(8): 18–21.

Cooper, B. 1984. *The End of History: An Essay on Modern Hegelianism.* Toronto: University of Toronto Press.

Craycraft, K. R. 1991. The Pope Embraces Market Economics. *World and I* 6 (11): 480–95.

Cvijić, J. 1931. *Balkansko Polustrvo i Jugoslavenske Zemlje.* Belgrade.

Danforth, K. C. 1990. Yugoslavia: A House Much Divided. *National Geographic* 178 (2): 92–123.

Djilas, A. 1991. *The Contested Country: Yugoslav Unity and Communist Revolution.* Cambridge: Harvard University Press.

Dostoevsky, F. 1976. *The Brothers Karamazov.* New York: Norton.

Drucker, P. 1990. Making Managers of Communism's Bureaucrats. *Wall Street Journal,* August 15, p. A-10.

Durkheim, E. [1893] 1993. *The Division of Labor in Society.* Translated by George Simpson. New York: Free Press.

———. [1895] 1982. The Rules of Sociological Method. In *Durkheim: The Rules of Sociological Method and Selected Texts on Sociology and Its Method,* edited by S. Lukes, pp. 31–163. New York: Free Press.

———. [1897] 1951. *Suicide: A Study in Sociology.* Translated by John A. Spaulding and George Simpson. New York: Free Press.

———. [1912] 1965. *The Elementary Forms of the Religious Life.* Translated by J. Swain. New York: Free Press.

———. [1914] 1973. The Dualism of Human Nature and Its Social Conditions. In *Emile Durkheim on Morality and Society,* edited by R. Bellah, pp. 149–66. Chicago: University of Chicago Press.

———. 1915. *Germany above All.* Paris: Armand Collin.

———. 1928. *Le Socialisme.* Paris: Retz.

———. [1950] 1983. *Professional Ethics and Civic Morals.* Translated by Cornelia Brookfield. Westport, Conn.: Greenwood Press.

———. 1980. *Emile Durkheim: Contributions to L'Année Sociologique.* Edited by Y. Nandan. New York: Free Press.

———. 1986. *Durkheim on Politics and the State.* Edited by A. Giddens. London: Polity.

Dvorniković, D. 1931. *Karakaterologija Jugoslavena.* Belgrade.

Eberstadt, N. 1987. *The Poverty of Communism.* New Brunswick, N.J.: Transaction.

———. 1990. Europe's Border between Sickness and Health. *Wall Street Journal,* April 6, p. A-6.

Edynak, G. J.; Bartel, B.; Compton, C. B.; et al. 1976. A Test of a Migration Hypothesis: Slavic Movements into the Karst Region of Yugoslavia. *Current Anthropology* 17 (3): 413–19.

Elias, N. 1982. *The Civilizing Process.* Oxford: Basil Blackwell.

Ellenberger, H. 1970. *The Discovery of the Unconscious.* New York: Basic Books.

Etzioni, A. 1988. *The Moral Dimension: Toward a New Economics.* New York: Free Press.

————. 1991a. American Competitiveness: The Moral Dimension. *World and I* 6 (10): 465–73.

————. 1991b. Eastern Eruope: The Wealth of Lessons. *Challenge,* July/August, pp. 4–10.

————. 1991c. A New Community of Thinkers, both Liberal and Conservative. *Wall Street Journal,* August 16, p. A-20.

Fauconnet, P. 1920. *La Responsabilité: Etude sociologique.* Paris: Alcan.

Featherstone, M. 1988. In Pursuit of the Postmodern: An Introduction. *Theory, Culture, and Society* 5 (2–3): 195–216.

————. 1990. *Global Culture: Nationalism, Globalization, and Modernity.* London: Sage.

Ferfila, B. 1991. Yugoslavia: Confederation or Disintegration? *Problems of Communism* 40:18–30.

Forman, C. 1991. Soviet Economy Holds Potential for Disaster As the Union Weakens: Various Republics Squabble over Assets Though They Are Very Interdependent. *Wall Street Journal,* September 4, p. A-1.

Freud, S. [1901] 1965. *The Psychopathology of Everyday Life.* New York: Norton.

Frisby, D. 1986. *Fragments of Modernity.* Cambridge: MIT Press.

Fromm, E. 1947. *Man for Himself.* New York: Rinehart.

————. 1950. *Psychoanalysis and Religion.* New Haven: Yale University Press.

————. 1955. *The Sane Society.* Greenwich, Conn.: Fawcett.

————. 1962. *Beyond the Chains of Illusion.* New York: Simon & Schuster.

————. 1963. *The Dogma of Christ and Other Essays on Religion, Psychology, and Culture.* New York: Holt, Rinehart, and Winston.

————. 1964. *The Heart of Man: Its Genius for Good and Evil.* New York: Harper.

Fromm, E., and M. Maccoby. 1970. *Social Character in a Mexican Village: A Sociopsychoanalytic Study.* Englewood Cliffs, N.J.: Prentice-Hall.

Fukuyama, F. 1989. The End of History? *National Interest* 16 (Summer): 3–19.

———. 1990. *A Look at "The End of History?"* Washington, D.C.: U.S. Institute of Peace.

———. 1991. Are We at the End of History? *Fortune,* January 15, pp. 75–77.

———. 1992. *The End of History and the Last Man.* New York: Free Press.

Gagnon, V. P. 1991. Yugoslavia: Prospects for Stability. *Foreign Affairs* 70 (3): 17–35.

Galbraith, J. K., and S. Menshikov. 1988. *Capitalism, Communism, and Coexistence.* Boston: Houghton.

Gallais, J. 1972. The West African Pastoral Societies in the Face of Development. *Cahiers d'Etudes Africaines* 12 (3): 353–68.

Gane, M. 1991. *Baudrillard: Critical and Fatal Theory.* London: Routledge.

Gastil, R. D. 1971. Homicide and a Regional Culture of Violence. *American Sociological review* 36 (June): 412–27.

Giddens, A. 1970. Durkheim as a Review Critic. *Sociological Review* 18:171–96.

———. 1977. *Studies in Social and Political Theory.* New York: Basic.

———. 1982. *A Contemporary Critique of Historical Materialism.* Berkeley: University of California Press.

———. 1987. *Social Theory and Modern Sociology.* Stanford: Stanford University Press.

———. 1990. *The Consequences of Modernity.* Stanford: Stanford University Press.

———. 1991. *Modernity and Self-Identity.* Stanford: Stanford University Press.

———. 1992. Uprooted Signposts at Century's End. *The Higher* January 17, p. 21.

Glenny, M. 1992. The Massacre of Yugoslavia. *New York Review of Books* 39 (3): 30–34.

Glynn, P. 1992. Yugoblunder. *New Republic,* February 24, pp. 15–17.

Goldfarb, J. 1989. *Beyond Glasnost: The Post-totalitarian Mind*. Chicago: University of Chicago Press.

Golitsyn, A. 1984. *New Lies for Old*. New York: Dodd, Mead.

Gorbachev, M. S. 1986a. *The Challenge of Our Time: Disarmament and Social Progress*. New York: International Publishers.

———. 1986b. *The Coming Century of Peace*. New York: Richardson & Steirman.

———. 1987. *Perestroika: New Thinking for Our Country and the World*. New York: Harper & Row.

———. 1992. No Time for Stereotypes. *New York Times*, February 24, p. A-13.

Gripkey, M. 1969. *The Blessed Virgin Mary as Mediatrix*. New York: AMS Press.

Gruenwald, O. 1983. *The Yugoslav Search for Man: Marxist Humanism in Contemporary Yugoslavia*. South Hadley, Mass.: J. Bergin Press.

———. 1990. The Icon in Russian Art, Society, and Culture. In *Christianity and Russian Culture in Soviet Society*, edited by N. N. Petro, pp. 161–82. Boulder, Colo.: Westview.

Gumbel, P. 1991. The Vodka Putsch: How Not to Mount a Coup, the Lessons from the Kremlin—Booze, Lies, and Distrust Led Plotters into a Drama with Tragicomic Scenes. *Wall Street Journal*, August 29, p. A-1.

Habermas, J. 1970. *Legitimation Crisis*. Boston: Beacon.

———. 1981. Modernity versus Postmodernity. *New German Critique* 22:3–14.

———. 1987. *The Philosophical Discourse of Modernity*. Cambridge: MIT Press.

Hankiss, E. 1990. *East European Alternatives*. Oxford: Clarendon.

Harvey, D. 1989. *The Condition of Postmodernity*. London: Basil Blackwell.

Harwood, J. 1991. Surveyed Americans Believe Soviet Communism Is Dead but Don't Want to Fund Economic Rescue. *Wall Street Journal*, August 30, p. A-8.

Hegel, G. W. F. [1899] 1965. *The Philosophy of History*. New York: Dover.

Helsinki Watch Committee. 1982. *Yugoslavia: Freedom to Conform*. New York: U.S. Helsinki Watch Committee.

———. 1990. *Yugoslavia: Crisis in Kosovo*. New York: U.S. Helsinki Watch Committee.

———. 1991a. *Human Rights Abuses in the Croatian Conflict*. New York: U.S. Helsinki Watch Committee.

———. 1991b. *March 1991 Demonstrations in Belgrade*. New York: U.S. Helsinki Watch Committee.

———. 1992a. *Open Letter to President Franjo Tudjman of Croatia, February 13*. New York: U.S. Helsinki Watch Committee.

———. 1992b. *Open Letter to President Slobodan Milošević of Serbia, January 21*. New York: U.S. Helsinki Watch Committee.

Herolt, J. 1928. *Miracles of the Blessed Virgin Mary*. New York: Harcourt, Brace.

Hertz, R. [1907–1909] 1960. *Death and the Right Hand*. Aberdeen, Scotland: Cohen & West.

Hollander, P. 1988. *The Survival of Adversary Culture: Social Criticism and Political Escapism in American Society*. New Brunswick, N.J.: Transaction Books.

Holsti, K. J. 1991. *Peace and War: Armed Conflicts and International Order, 1648–1989*. Cambridge: Cambridge University Press.

Holub, R. C. 1991. *Jürgen Habermas: Critic in the Public Sphere*. London: Routledge.

Honigman, J. J. 1949. Review of *Personality and Culture in Eastern European Politics*, by D. Tomašić. *Social Forces* 28 (3): 349.

Horkheimer, M., and Adorno, T. 1972. *Dialectic of Enlightenment*. New York: Continuum Publishing.

Horowitz, I. L. 1982. Socialization without Politicization. *Political Theory* 10:353–78.

Humphrey, C. 1989. Perestroika and the Pastoralists: The Example of Mongun-Taiga in Tuva. *Anthropology Today* 5 (3): 6–10.

James, W. [1890] 1950. *The Principles of Psychology.* New York: Longmans.

Janaway, C. 1989. *Self and World in Schopenhauer's Philosophy.* New York: Oxford.

Judas, M. 1992. *Mass Killing and Genocide in Croatia, 1991–1992.* Zagreb: National Ministry of Information.

Kalberg, S. 1985. Max Weber. In *The Social Science Encyclopedia,* edited by A. Kuper and J. Kuper, pp. 892–96. London: Routledge.

———. 1987. The Origin and Expansion of *Kulturpessimismus:* The Relationship between Public and Private Spheres in Early Twentieth Century Germany. *Sociological Theory* 5:150–65.

———. 1989. The Federal Republic at Forty: A Burdened Democracy? *German Politics and Society* 16:33–40.

———. 1991. The Hidden Link between Internal Political Culture and Cross-national Perceptions: Divergent Images of the Soviet Union in the US and the Federal Republic of Germany. *Theory, Culture, and Society* 8 (2): 31–55.

Kanter, D. L., and Mirvis, P. H. 1989. *The Cynical Americans.* San Francisco: Jossey-Bass.

Kaplan, R. D. 1991. History's Cauldron. *Atlantic Monthly,* June, pp. 93–104.

Karan, M. 1973. Blood Vengeance: "Pathological" or "Normal" Behavior? *Sociologija* 15 (1): 117–36.

———. 1974a. The Rugovska Charter: An Example of Self-Management in the Control of Vendetta in a Kosovo Village. *Sociologija Sela* 12 (2–3): 28–36.

———. 1974b. Sociological and Psychological Aspects of the Ethnological Study of Bloods Feuds. *Sociologija* 16 (3–4): 453–72.

———. 1977. Psychological Aspects of Interdisciplinary Research of the Blood Feud. *Socioloski Pregled* 11 (2–3): 51–58.

———. 1983. Pleqnia as the Traditional Dispute Settlement Institution of the Albanians in Kosovo. *Socioloski Pregled* 17 (1–2): 115–27.

Karlović, N. L. 1982. Internal Colonialism in a Marxist Society: The Case of Croatia. *Ethnic and Racial Studies* 5:276–99.

Käsler, D. 1988. *Max Weber.* Chicago: University of Chicago Press.

Kellner D. 1988. Postmodernism as Social Theory. *Theory, Culture, and Society* 5:239–70.

———. 1989. *Jean Baudrillard: From Marxism to Postmodernism and Beyond.* Stanford: Stanford University Press.

Kempe, F. 1990. After the Euphoria: Specter of Capitalism Haunts East Germans Used to Certainties—Prospect of Layoffs, Inequities, and Meager Means Causes Anxiety and Bitterness. *Wall Street Journal,* June 14, p. A-1.

Kimball, R. 1992. Review of *The Disuniting of America,* by A. Schlesinger, Jr. *Wall Street Journal,* February 21.

Klaić, N. 1978. Principles of Association in Croatia in the Early Middle Ages. *Sociologija Sela* 16:104–10.

Kroker, A., and Cook, D. 1986. *The Postmodern Scene: Excremental Culture and Hyper-Aesthetics.* New York: St. Martin's Press.

Kroker, A., and Kroker, M. 1991. *Ideology and Power in the Age of Lenin in Ruins.* New York: St. Martin's Press.

Lacroix, B. 1979. The Elementary Forms of Religious Life as a Reflection of Power. *Critique of Anthropology* 4:87–103.

———. 1981. *Durkheim et la politique.* Montreal: Presses de l'Université de Montreal.

Lasch, C. 1979. *The Culture of Narcissism.* New York: Norton.

———. 1991. *The True and Only Heaven: Progress and Its Critics.* New York: Norton.

Lendvai, P. 1991. Yugoslavia without Yugoslavs: The Roots of the Crisis. *International Affairs* 67:252–61.

Letica, S. 1988. *Intelektualac i Kriza.* Zagreb: August Cesarec.

———. 1989. *Četvrta Jugoslavija.* Zagreb: Dnevnik.

———. 1990. Jesu li Dinarci Trajno Konvertibilni. *Start,* April 28, pp. 32–33.

———. 1992. *Obečana Zemlja.* Zagreb: Biblioteka Leonem.

Lipset, S. M. 1989. *The Continental Divide.* London: Routledge.

Lott, D., and Hart, B. 1977. Aggressive Domination of Cattle by Fulani Herdsmen and its Relation to Aggression in Fulani Culture and Personality. *Ethos* 5 (2): 174–88.

Lotz, J. 1992. The Kosice Connection. In *Proceedings of the International Colloquium on Regional Development: Problems of Countries in Transition to a Market Economy*. Frankfurt: Springer Verlag.

Lucev, I. 1974. Social Character and Political Culture. *Sociologija* 16 (1): 23–44.

Luft, E. 1988. *Schopenhauer: New Essays in Honor of His Two Hundredth Birthday*. Lewiston, N.Y.: Mellen.

Lukàcs, G. 1980. *The Destruction of Reason*. Translated by Peter Palmer. Atlantic Highlands, N.J.: Humanities Press.

Lukes, S. 1985. *Emile Durkheim*. Stanford: Stanford University Press.

Lyotard, J. 1984. *The Postmodern Condition*. Minneapolis: University of Minnesota Press.

Machotka, O. 1949. Review of *Personality and Culture in Eastern European Politics*, by D. Tomašić. *American Journal of Sociology* 55 (1): 104–106.

McLellan, D. 1987. *Marxism and Religion*. New York: Harper & Row.

Magee, B. 1983. *The Philosophy of Schopenhauer*. New York: Oxford University Press.

Mallock, W. 1989. *A Critical Examination of Socialism*. New Brunswick, N.J.: Transaction.

Mamchur, S. W. 1949. Review of *Personality and Culture in Eastern European Politics*, by D. Tomašić. *American Sociological Review* 14 (2): 326.

Mathisen, J. A. 1989. Twenty Years after Bellah: Whatever Happened to American Civil Religion? *Sociological Analysis* 50 (2): 29–46.

Merelman, R. M. 1991. *Partial Visions: Culture and Politics in Britain, Canada, and the United States*. Madison: University of Wisconsin Press.

Merton, R. K. 1957. *Social Theory and Social Structure*. New York: Free Press.

Meštrović, S. G. 1982. In the Shadow of Plato: Durkheim and Freud on Suicide and Society. Ph.D. diss., Syracuse University.

————. 1988. Emile Durkheim and the Reformation of Sociology. Totowa, N.J.: Rowman & Littlefield.

————. 1991. The Coming Fin de Siècle: An Application of Durkheim's Sociology to Modernity and Postmodernism. London: Routledge.

————. 1992. Durkheim and Postmodern Culture. Hawthorne, N.Y.: Aldine de Gruyter.

Meštrović, S. G.; Goreta, M.; and Letica, S. 1993. The Road from Paradise. Lexington: University Press of Kentucky.

Mitrović, M. 1982. Dinko Tomašić. In Predratna Sociologija, pp. 169–83. SSO Srbije.

Molnar, T. 1967. Utopia: The Perennial Heresy. New York: Sheed & Ward.

Mumford, L. 1955. The Human Prospect. Boston: Beacon.

Muravchick, J. 1991. Exporting Democracy: Fulfilling America's Destiny. Washington, D.C.: American Enterprise Institute Press.

Murvar, V. 1982. Submerged Nations: An Invitation to Theory. Milwaukee: Max Weber Symposia.

Nandan, Y. 1980. Emile Durkheim: Contributions to L'Année Sociologique. New York: Free Press.

Nelson, M. 1990. Darkness at Noon: As Shroud of Secrecy Lifts in East Europe, Smog Shroud Emerges. Wall Street Journal, March 10, p. A-6.

Nietzsche, F. [1874] 1965. Schopenhauer as Educator. South Bend, Ind.: Gateway.

Nixon, R. 1991. How the West Can Bring Peace to Yugoslavia. Wall Street Journal, December 17, p. A-12.

————. 1992a. The Challenge We Face in Russia. Wall Street Journal, March 11.

————. 1992b. Seize the Moment: America's Challenge in a One-Superpower World. New York: Simon & Schuster.

Novak, M. 1982. The Spirit of Democratic Capitalism. New York: Simon & Schuster.

————. 1991. Transforming the Democratic/Capitalist Revolution. Paper presented at the Karl Brunner Symposium, Interlaken, Switzerland.

Paige, J. 1974. Kinship and Polity in Stateless Societies. *American Journal of Sociology* 80:301–20.

Parsons, T. 1937. *The Structure of Social Action.* Glencoe, Ill.: Free Press.

Pearce, F. 1989. *The Radical Durkheim.* London: Unwin Hyman.

Pecjak, V. 1992. *How Communism Collapsed: A Psychosocial Analysis of Events in Socialist Countries.* Ljubljana, Slovenia: Samozalozba.

Peet, R. 1991. The End of History . . . or Its Beginning? *Professional Geographer* 43:512–19.

Petak, A. 1974. An Approach to Regional Differentiation at the Eighth Professional Meeting of Yugoslav Sociologists. *Revija za Sociologiju* 4 (2–3): 87–97.

Petro, N. 1990. *Christianity and Russian Culture in Soviet Society.* Boulder, Colo.: Westview Press.

Pilon, J. G. 1992. Post-Communist Nationalism: The Case of Romania. *World and I* 7 (2): 110–15.

Popović, T. 1988. *Prince Marko: The Hero of the South Slavic Epics.* Syracuse: Syracuse University Press.

Prager, J. 1981. Moral Integration and Political Inclusion: A Comparison of Durkheim's and Weber's Theories of Democracy. *Social Forces* 59:918–50.

Prpić, G. J. 1982. *Croatia and the Croatians: A Selected and Annotated Bibliography in English.* Scottsdale, Ariz.: Associated Book Publishers.

Ramet, P. 1987. *Cross and Commissar: The Politics of Religion in Eastern Europe and the USSR.* Bloomington: Indiana University Press.

Richter, M. 1960. Durkheim's Politics and Political Theory. In *Emile Durkheim, 1858–1917,* edited by K. Wolff, pp. 170–210. Columbus: Ohio State University Press.

Riesman, D. [1950] 1977. *The Lonely Crowd*. New Haven: Yale University Press.

———. 1953. *Thorstein Veblen: A Critical Interpretation*. New York: Charles Scribner's Sons.

———. 1954. *Individualism Reconsidered*. Glencoe, Ill.: Free Press.

———. 1964. *Abundance for What?* Garden City, N.Y.: Doubleday.

———. 1976. Liberation and Stalemate. *Massachusetts Review* 17 (4): 767–76.

———. 1977. Prospects for Human Rights. *Society* 15 (1): 28–33.

———. 1980a. Egocentrism. *Character* 1 (5): 3–9.

———. 1980b. *On Higher Education: The Academic Enterprise in an Era of Rising Student Consumerism*. San Francisco: Jossey-Bass.

———. 1981. The Dream of Abundance Reconsidered. *Public Opinion Quarterly* 45 (3): 285–302.

———. 1990. The Innocence of the *Lonely Crowd*. *Society* 27 (2): 76–79.

Riesman, D., and Riesman, E. T. 1967. *Conversations in Japan: Modernization, Politics, and Culture*. Chicago: University of Chicago Press.

Rojek, C. 1985. *Capitalism and Leisure Theory*. London: Tavistock.

Rosenau, P. M. 1992. *Post-Modernism and the Social Sciences: Insights, Inroads, and Intrusions*. Princeton: Princeton University Press.

Rotfeld, A. D., and Stutzle, W. 1991. *Germany and Europe in Transition*. New York: Oxford.

Ryan, A. 1992. Review of *The End of History and the Last Man*, by F. Fukuyama. *New York Review of Books*, March 26, pp. 7–12.

Saint Erlich, V. 1973. Cultural Traditions in Rural Yugoslavia. *Sociologija* 15 (3–4): 609–17.

———. 1974. Regional Differences and Emotional Climate. *Sociologija* 16 (1): 61–72.

Scales, J. I. 1987. *Cause at Heart: A Former Communist Remembers*. Athens: University of Georgia Press.

Schneider, D. M. 1957. Review of *National Communism and Soviet Strategy*, by D. Tomašić. *American Sociological Review* 22 (4): 493–94.

Schneider, L. 1948. *The Freudian Psychology and Veblen's Social Theory*. Morningside Heights, N.Y.: King's Crown Press.

Schoenfeld, C. G. 1962. God the Father-and-Mother: Study and Extension of Freud's Conception of God as an Exalted Father. *American Imago* 19 (3): 213–34.

————. 1966. Erich Fromm's Attacks upon the Oedipus Complex — a Brief Critique. *Journal of Nervous and Mental Disease* 141 (5): 580–85.

————. 1968. Psychoanalytic Guideposts for the Good Society. *Psychoanalytic Review* (Spring): 91–114.

————. 1974. International Law, Nationalism, and the Sense of Self: A Psychoanalytic Inquiry. *Journal of Psychiatry and Law* (Fall): 303–17.

————. 1984. *Psychoanalysis Applied to the Law*. Port Washington, N.Y.: Associated Faculty Press.

————. 1988. Blacks and Violent Crime: A Psychoanalytically Oriented Analysis. *Journal of Psychiatry and Law* (Summer): 269–301.

————. 1991. Holmmes v. Bork: The Role of Unconscious Thoughts and Emotions in Law and the Politics of Law. *Political Psychology* 12 (2): 363–75.

Schoenfeld, E. 1987. Militant Religion. In *Religious Society*, edited by W. Swatos, pp. 125–37. Westport, Conn.: Greenwood Press.

Schoenfeld, E., and Meštrović, S. G. 1989. Durkheim's Concept of Justice and Its Relationship to Social Solidarity. *Sociological Analysis* 50 (2): 111–27.

————. 1991. With Justice and Mercy: Instrumental-Masculine and Expressive-Feminine Elements in Religion. *Journal for the Scientific Study of Religion* 30 (4): 363–80.

Schoffeleers, M., and Meijers, D. 1978. *Religion, Nationalism, and Economic Action: Critical Questions on Durkheim and Weber*. Assen, Holland: Van Goreum.

Schopenhauer, A. [1818] 1969. *The World as Will and Representation*. translated by E. Payne. 2 vols. New York: Dover Press.

――――. [1841] 1965. *On the Basis of Morality*. Indianapolis: Bobbs-Merrill.

Scrinton, R. 1988. Spengler's Decline of the West. *World and I* 3 (9): 548–67.

Simmel, G. [1907] 1986. *Schopenhauer and Nietzsche*. Amherst: University of Massachusetts Press.

Skrbić, M.; Letica, S.; Popović, B.; Butković, J.; and Matutinović, A. 1984. *Socijalna Zastita*. Zagreb: Jugoslavenska Medicinska Naklada.

Sloterdijk, P. 1987. *Critique of Cynical Reason*. Translated by Michael Eldred. Minneapolis: University of Minnesota Press.

Smith, A. D. 1983. Nationalism and Classical Social Theory. *British Journal of Sociology* 34:19–38.

――――. 1986 *The Ethnic Origins of Nations*. London: Basil Blackwell.

Sorokin, P. 1944. *Russia and the United States*. New York: E. P. Dutton.

――――. 1947. *The Ways and Power of Love*. New York: American Book Company.

――――. 1948. *The Reconstruction of Humanity*. Boston: Beacon.

――――. 1950. *Altruistic Love*. Boston: Beacon.

――――. 1957. *Social and Cultural Dynamics*. New York: American Book Company.

――――. 1963. *A Long Journey: The Autobiography of Pitirim A. Sorokin*. New Haven: College and University Press.

Sowell, T. 1991. Cultural Diversity: A World View. *The American Enterprise* 2:44–55.

Spengler, O. [1926] 1961. *The Decline of the West*. New York: Alfred A. Knopf.

Staar, R. 1988. *Communist Regimes in Eastern Europe*. Stanford: Hoover Institute Press.

Stamac, A. 1992. Hrvatski Novi Aktivizam. *Danas*, December 11, p. 1.

Stark, D. 1992. Path Dependence and Privatization Strategies in East-

Central Europe. *East European Politics and Societies* 6 (1): 17–52.

Stark, R. 1991. *Sociology: An Introduction*. Belmont, Calif.: Wadsworth.

Stojsavljević, B. 1974. Some Data on the Economic Families and Their Disintegration. *Sociologija* 12 (1): 63–70.

Stulhofer, A. 1992. Dinko Tomašić: Modern Sociologist. Paper presented to the Croatian Sociological Association, February 5, at Zagreb, Croatia.

Szelenyi, I. 1988. *Socialist Entrepreneurs: Embourgeoisement in Rural Hungary*. Madison: University of Wisconsin Press.

Szporluk, R. 1988. *Communism and Nationalism*. New York: Oxford.

Tagliabue, J. 1991. Old Tribal Rivalries in Eastern Europe Pose Threat of Infection. *New York Times*, October 13, p. 2.

Thurow, R. 1991a. Exorcism in Moscow Does Little to Banish Ghost of Ceauşescu: Many Romanians See in Coup Evidence His Spirit Lives; "Come Out of Your Grave." *Wall Street Journal*, September 4, p. A-1.

———. 1991b. Past Horrors Shadow Riven Yugoslavia: Fights of 1940s Stoke "Second Second World War." *Wall Street Journal*, November 27, p. A-6.

Timascheff, N. S. 1953. Review of *The Impact of Russian Culture on Soviet Communism*, by D. Tomašić. *American Sociological Review* 18 (3): 725–26.

Tiryakian, E. A. 1980. Quebec, Wales, and Scotland: Three Nations in Search of a State. *International Journal of Comparative Sociology* 21:1–13.

———. 1985. *New Nationalisms of the Developed West: Toward Explanation*. Boston: Allen & Unwin.

———. 1988. Sociology's Dostoevski: Pitirim A. Sorokin. *World and I* 3 (9): 568–81.

Tismaneanu, V. 1988. *The Crisis of Marxist Ideology in Eastern Europe*. London: Routledge.

Tocqueville, A. [1845] 1945. *Democracy in America*. Vol. 1. New York: Random House.

Toffler, A. 1980. *The Third Wave.* New York: William Morrow.

Tomašić, D. 1941. Sociology in Yugoslavia. *American Journal of Sociology* 47:53–69.

———. 1946. The Structure of Balkan Society. *American Journal of Sociology* 52:132–40.

———. 1948a. Ideologies and the Structure of Eastern European Society. *American Journal of Sociology* 53:367–75.

———. 1948b. *Personality and Culture in Eastern European Politics.* New York: George Stewart Publishers.

———. 1951. Interrelations between Bolshevik Ideology and the Structure of Soviet Society. *American Sociological Review* 16: 137–48.

———. 1953. *The Impact of Russian Culture on Soviet Communism.* Glencoe, Ill.: Free Press.

Tönnies, F. [1887] 1963. *Community and Society.* New York: Harper & Row.

———. [1921] 1974. *Karl Marx: His Life and Teachings.* Translated by C. Loomis and I. Paulus. East Lansing: Michigan State University Press.

Toynbee, A. 1962. *America and the World Revolution.* New York: Oxford.

———. 1978. *Arnold Toynbee: A Selection from His Works.* Edited by C. Tomlin. Oxford: Oxford University Press.

Tudjman, F. 1981. *Nationalism in Contemporary Europe.* New York: Columbia University Press.

Veblen, T. [1899] 1967. *The Theory of the Leisure Class.* New York: Penguin.

———. [1915] 1964. *Imperial Germany and the Industrial Revolution.* New York: Sentry Press.

———. 1917. *An Inquiry into the Nature of Peace and the Terms of Its Perpetuation.* New York: Macmillan.

———. 1943. *Essays in Our Changing Order.* New York: Viking.

Veselica, M. 1980. *The Croatian National Question—Yugoslavia's Achilles Heel.* London: United Publishers.

Viorst, M. 1991. The Yugoslav Idea. *New Yorker,* March 18, pp. 58–79.

Warhola, J. W. 1992. *The Religious Dimension of Ethnic Conflict in the Soviet Union*. International Journal of Politics, Culture, and Society 5 (2): 1–17.

Weber, E. 1987. *France, Fin de Siècle*. Cambridge: Harvard University Press.

Weber, M. [1904] 1958a. *The Protestant Ethic and the Spirit of Capitalism*. New York: Scribner's.

————. 1958b. *From Max Weber: Essays in Sociology*. Edited by H. H. Gerth and C. W. Mills. New York: Oxford.

Whiting, J. W., and Whiting, B. B. 1975. Aloofness and Intimacy of Husbands and Wives: A Cross-Cultural Study. *Ethos* 3 (2): 183–207.

Index